UNRAVELING THE MYSTERIES OF MYSTICISM

UNRAVELING THE MYSTERIES OF MYSTICISM

Six Philosophical Attacks on Mystics' Claims and Responses

Randall Firestone

The Edwin Mellen Press
Lewiston•Queenston•Lampeter

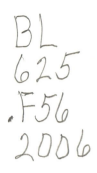
Library of Congress Cataloging-in-Publication Data

Firestone, Randall S.
  Unraveling the mysteries of mysticism : six philosophical attacks on mystics claims and
responses / Randall S. Firestone.
    p. cm.
  Includes bibliographical references and index.
  ISBN 0-7734-5905-7
  1. Mysticism. 2. Experience (Religion) 3. Religion--Controversial literature. I. Title.

BL625.F56 2006
204'.22--dc22

                                                                    2006041893

hors série.

A CIP catalog record for this book is available from the British Library.

        The Edwin Mellen Press   The Edwin Mellen Press
              Box 450   Box 67
        Lewiston, New York   Queenston, Ontario
         USA 14092-0450   CANADA L0S 1L0

                    The Edwin Mellen Press, Ltd.
                    Lampeter, Ceredigion, Wales
                    UNITED KINGDOM SA48 8LT

                 Printed in the United States of America

For my parents

Dr. William and Roberta Firestone

Table of Contents

Preface

Mysticism is the poetry of the soul. Some of the greatest thinkers and artists, religious and non-religious, have acknowledged that it provides an insight into reality and a profundity of feeling that count among the most valuable achievements of the human spirit. That is why there has always been a steady interest in the lives, utterances, and writings of mystics, even at times, perhaps especially at times, when institutional religion has been looked at with suspicion. The perception has been that mystics, because of their direct encounter with the Transcendent—which is rarer than is often imagined—provide us with the living and true heart of religion, and in the case of nature mysticism, with a window into the mysteries of the cosmos.

Philosophy, which tries to make conceptual sense of things, is faced with a challenge when it tries to explain mysticism. On the one hand, philosophy deals centrally with questions of meaning and truth and so is led naturally to examine mystical experience, which makes strong claims in those directions. On the other hand, this is difficult because mysticism goes beyond the bounds of ordinary experience and of the concepts and categories used to account for it. As Firestone says, mystical experiences are indeed "limit experiences". One may call them experiences because they are often clearly remembered and described, and yet the explanatory structures used to account for most experiences are often inadequate in the case of mystical encounters. This has led many either to explain them away, as in the reductive accounts of Freud or Nietzsche, or to claim that philosophy must be silent in the face of something that goes beyond its proper boundaries, as in Wittgenstein's famous warning: "Whereof one cannot speak, thereof one must be silent."

Wittgenstein, or at least the early Wittgenstein, was interested in articulating the structure of a logically perspicuous language, but argued that logical propositions "can express nothing that is higher" (*Tractatus* 6.42). The entire realm of "the higher," that is, statements of metaphysics, ethics, and religion, lies beyond the realm of propositional language. Based on their divergent interpretations of that judgment, Wittgenstein and his colleagues in the Vienna Circle came to radically different conclusions. They wanted to dismiss the discourse of ethics and religion as nonsensical and focus on logic and science, whereas Wittgenstein took exactly the opposite tack and argued that it was "the higher" that merited our deepest attention. It was this strong conviction that led the later Wittgenstein to develop a more pragmatic theory of language based on the deployment of different kinds of language games and the forms of life associated with them. While he did not analyze mysticism as such, dealing as he did more broadly with religious language, Wittgenstein said enough to make it clear that it is wiser to examine the special language of mysticism rather than to dismiss it *a priori* as incoherent or to assimilate it to conventional spatio-temporal experience.

In this excellent work, Randall Firestone implicitly follows the lead of the later Wittgenstein without explicitly invoking him. Not only does he examine and analyze the broad pattern of mystical statements, but he goes further in suggesting that they are perhaps "more true" than our statements rooted in mundane existence, touching as they do on a reality that may well be regarded as the ground or source of our being. Plato's notion of the Divided Line in the *Republic* introduces the idea that there are hierarchical levels of reality with images at the lowest rung, ascending through sense-objects, mathematical realities, and Forms at the highest level. Corresponding to these objects are modes of knowledge with image-making at the bottom, proceeding upwards through opinion, reasoning, and *noesis* or intuitive understanding at the top. Each mode of knowledge is associated with a certain mental act, with image-making being the most scattered and discrete and *noesis* being the most unified and integrative. Plotinus extends this Platonic ontology and epistemology to the One, the transcendent source of all being, which overcoming all subject-object dualisms functions as self-thinking Thought.

Firestone does not, however, assume or dogmatically assert the ontological priority of the mystical One. He arrives at it dialectically and that, in my opinion, is one of the great merits of his work. He is aware that in a scientific and empirical age, the very idea of the mystical is looked upon with skepticism. What scientific verification is there of mystical claims? Firestone demonstrates that the very question prejudges the issue in assuming that all realities must be either empirical or historico-cultural. But having pointed that out, he does not commit the same error in the opposite direction by straightforwardly assuming the existence of transcendent realities. Instead, in an open-ended investigative manner, he patiently refutes some of the pervasive and most powerful objections to mysticism. In particular, he rebuts the influential view of Steven Katz that all experience is culturally mediated. This is arguably untrue because there are substantial reports of pure, contentless experiences, and Firestone shows how it is possible for this to be the case at the earlier descriptive, phenomenological stage while allowing for cultural mediation at the later interpretative level. Within the canons of scientific explanation, this is a far more satisfactory hypothesis than Katz's peremptory and *a priori* dismissal of all unmediated experiences. The meditative "emptiness" techniques characteristic of some schools of Buddhism provide precisely the deconditioning of which Katz seems to either be unaware or to implicitly and thereby summarily reject.

Having effectively answered most of the common objections to the possibility and coherence of mystical experience, Firestone moves to discussing its objectivity and truth. Here too his approach is impeccably philosophical: "This book is a call for philosophers to look with an open mind at the possible explanations for the source of the mystical experience and to ponder what is the best explanation of the source of those experiences." Not only do we have a very broad spectrum of mystical reports spanning cultures and historical periods, but what is equally interesting are the common characteristics these reports share. These characteristics do not point to the strict identity of the diverse metaphysical experiences encountered. Each mystic unquestionably tends to interpret his experience in the light of his cultural background, and yet there is a remarkable family resemblance among these diverse descriptions. This in itself, as Firestone points out, does not guarantee the veridicality of mystical experiences, but at the very least it signals a strong presumption in that direction.

From a philosophical point of view, the "limit experience" of mysticism points both to the postulated character of the limits and to what may lie beyond them. In our age of science and empiricism, the limits of what is taken to be intelligible experiences are conditioned by assumptions about spatio-temporal existence. Beyond those limits, as Kant, like Wittgenstein after him, argued, we lapse into empty speculation in contrast to discursive knowledge. And yet Kant was convinced of the existence of a noumenal realm that we can quite intelligibly think about, even though we cannot strictly speaking have knowledge about it. Indeed for Kant, such a noumenal realm was the basis of the moral law, and he too, like Wittgenstein, believed that such a realm could and should be "shown" even if not spoken about.

Non-western cultures, and indeed even the West before the advent of the modern scientific era, theorized quite differently about the limits of human experience. Thus, to mention just one example, the Upanishads in the Indian tradition see the Atman, the deep self within each person, as being the "real" self, and the empirical ego as an instrument or expression of Atman. The fundamental ontology is not that of discrete material entities but of Atman-Brahman, infinite unified consciousness, that expresses itself alike in the realms of the human, the divine, and the cosmic. This is not as fanciful a world-view as our contemporary empirical perspective would have us believe. Indeed, as J.N. Findlay argues in a long passage that Firestone cites: "[the] mystical unity at the limit or centre of things alone guarantees that coherence and continuity at the periphery, which is involved in all our basic rational enterprises."

It is widely imagined that the empirical temper of our age is determined by the strictures of modern science. All the more interesting, therefore, is the fact that much contemporary natural science is at the very least open and curious about the mystical world-view. From Werner Heisenberg and Ernst Schroedinger to Einstein and David Bohm, with others in between, many scientists have held that the unity and interdependence of the mystical point of view is a greatly appealing hypothesis, not just on aesthetic but also on scientific and philosophical grounds. To take one example, the attempt to arrive at a unified field theory where the basic forces of the universe are seen to be deeply interconnected, has scientists communicating with mystics and people of religion. Many conferences in recent times have prominent scientists coming together with people of religious faith. These developments point to a potentially new paradigm. Some of this new paradigm has been widely reported in such popular works as *The Tao of Physics* and *The Dancing Wu Li Masters*, but it is important to point out that these and other books publicize high-level and cutting-edge research.

One hopes that this book will enjoy a similar popularity. It is beautifully written with a directness and forcefulness often lacking in many academic works. I am greatly impressed by both the style and the substance of the book. In the process of tackling two central questions in the field of mysticism, it manages to shed light on many aspects of this vast terrain. While analyzing the nature of mystical experience, Firestone points to the fact that these experiences arise within the life of a person and that what matters are not isolated experiences so much as the unified life of which such experiences are tips of an iceberg, or to change the metaphor, occasional peaks appearing above the clouds hiding a vast mountain range. And while the work is rigorously philosophical in temper, it hints also at the limits of philosophy and the sagacity of John Keats' "negative capability," that is, "when man is capable of being in uncertainties, mysteries and doubts, without any irritable reaching after fact and reason." It is certainly a worthwhile enterprise to "unravel the mysteries of mysticism" while being aware that relative failure here might actually betoken wisdom.

Joseph Prabhu, Ph.D.
Professor of Philosophy
California State University, Los Angeles

Acknowledgments

I would first like to thank Professor Joseph Prabhu for not only writing the preface to this book, but also for being my mentor and, more importantly my friend. You continue to be an inspiration and provide me with a role model for what Aristotle's happy life looks like—one of accomplishment, fulfillment, respect from colleagues, and genuine friendships. I am also indebted to Professors Manuel Im and Jenny Faust for their invaluable feedback, comments and suggestions, and to Professor Matt Lawrence for taking the time to review the manuscript on relatively short notice.

Additionally, I wish to express my heartfelt affection and appreciation to two women who have been eager to read any and all philosophical papers I have written, and who have always been my biggest fans—my good friend, Mary Jelkes, and my mother, Roberta Firestone. I certainly must mention my father, William Firestone, who, in his strong, quiet and loving way, has always been the rock that I could count on to be there for wise and thoughtful counsel on virtually any subject. Lastly, I cannot pass on the opportunity to acknowledge my 10-year-old daughter, Kyra, who has not only allowed me to experience deep and unbounded love, but has also helped me understand the meaning of life, or should I say, has provided so much meaning to my life.

Foreword by the Author

In a world with so much violence, greed and cruelty, and with the ever-increasing availability of weapons of mass destruction, the mystics' message of unity and peace would seem to be needed now more than ever before. However good and important that message may be, there is a real question as to whether the claims made by various mystics are defensible. For example, is there an underlying unity to the world, and if so, is this unity more real than the multiplicity which we experience in everyday life? Do mystics really tap into truths that the rest of us have not seen or experienced?

If the mystical message is to be well-received, it would be helpful if the source and veracity of the claims made by the mystics are credible. Many recent philosophers, however, have questioned both the messenger and the message. So-called mystical truths about the world are perceived by these philosophers as outlandish and unsubstantiated claims due to an unintentional self-delusion on the part of the mystic. These philosophers are quite confident in their conclusions, and have all but declared victory, believing their analysis to be the last word on the subject.

This book analyzes the degree to which the recent philosophical challenges to the mystics' claims have been successful. It brings together the six major philosophical attacks on these claims, and then attempts to propose the best responses the mystic could provide. What emerges, I believe, is that the truth of the claims made by the mystics is still an open question. The philosophers have not in fact dealt the knockout punch that they have imagined. Probably the biggest reason for this is that they have failed to see that the majority of advanced mystical experiences involve different stages, and while their criticisms may be valid when applied to the last or later stages of the mystical experience, those criticisms would seem to hold no weight when applied to the earlier stages of contentlessness and unity.

If the analysis in this book is correct, then the reader is left to decide for himself what is the best explanation for the mystical experience: Is it due to a human predisposition or human make-up that generates, creates or manufactures such experiences under specific conditions? In the alternative, is there an external reality which the mystics are tapping into and is the source of their experiences? The answers to these questions are still unclear.

Randy Firestone

Chapter 1

Introduction: The Philosophical Debate About Mystical Experiences

A.   Why Mysticism Is Important

There have been mystics probably for as long as there have been humans. Even with the rise in education and concomitant decrease in superstition over the last 2,500 years, a relatively small amount of time in humanity's history, the mystical experience has had a disproportionate influence on the world compared with the relative paucity of people who claim to have had a mystical experience. Christianity, Judaism, Islam, Hinduism, Taoism, and Buddhism have all been either driven or significantly shaped by the influence of mystics, and these religions have been the driving forces of our history and our world for the past two millennia. The influence of the Christian Church in the Western world, and of Buddhist and Hindu teachings in the Eastern world, have permeated almost all aspects of society—affecting eating habits, business practices, leisure activities (such as charitable work, prayer, and meditation), and even whether there will be peace or war.

Many of the people we admire have either had mystical experiences, or seem to live their lives based on the concept of unity rather than duality—the principles of helping others, loving others, and living a life of peace. This unity is the most overriding and significant characteristic of the mystical experience, and will be elucidated in Chapters 2 and 3. Men such as Jesus Christ, the Buddha, Mahatma Gandhi, and Martin Luther King all lived and spoke in accord with the mystical experience of unity that was more real and more important to them than the duality and multiplicity that most people experience, feel and live. The Buddha's teachings came directly as a result of a mystical experience during meditation.

Mystical experiences have formed the basis for much of ethics. The Buddha

2

and Jesus Christ preached and taught how one could best live his or her life -- and this preaching was not based on intellectual, logical or practical formulations, but rather, on experience—the experience of unity over separation. Is it a coincidence that the major religious traditions all seem to stress the same general concepts that foster unity and love over selfishness and hate?

Many experts on mysticism have not been shy in pronouncing its influence and importance. For example, F.C. Happold, in his book titled *Mysticism*, proclaimed as follows:

> [A]ll the most profound insights of religious truth have their origin in the mystical experiences of those who have led the spiritual progress of the human race.[1]

S.N. Dasgupta, in the preface to his book *Hindu Mysticism*, boldly asserted:

> Mysticism is the basis of all religions— particularly of religion as it appears in the lives of truly religious men.[2]

The famous English philosopher Bertrand Russell recognized the important influence mysticism exercised on some of the greatest philosophers, including the ancient Greek philosophers Heraclitus and Plato—an influence that helped philosophy find its niche and its greatness beyond the domains of science and religion.

> But the greatest men who have been philosophers have felt the need both of science and of mysticism: the attempt to harmonize the two was what made their life, and what always must, for all its arduous uncertainty, make philosophy, to some minds, a greater thing than either science or religion.[3]

W.T. Stace, in his book, "Mysticism and Philosophy," points out how mysticism is the founding essence of the Eastern religions, with a lesser albeit important role in the West.

> We shall, of course, expect to find the paradoxes of mysticism expressed in their most extreme or violent form in those religions and philosophies in which mysticism is the major inspiring influence. And these are undoubtedly the religions and philosophies of India. Both the religion of the Upanishads and the philosophy of the

Vedanta are almost wholly founded on the mystical consciousness.
It is their supreme fountainhead. The same is true of Buddhism,
which is founded entirely upon the enlightenment experience of the
Buddha. In the Western theistic religions, mysticism is, as Professor
Burtt has said, a minor strain though an important one.[4]

It has been recognized that the mystical experience has been utilized as a
foundation for religious experience.

One issue is whether, like sense-data in classic philosophy of
perception, it provides an indubitable foundation for knowledge.
Thus, Gill writes, "Empiricist philosophers of the "foundationalist"
school . . . have long sought to ground experiential knowledge in
some form of awareness that is epistemologically certain, such as
sense-data reports. In its own way, mysticism represents a form of
foundationalism in that it seeks to ground religious awareness in an
incorrigible experience.[5]

In this age of science and rationality coupled with doses of skepticism and
atheism, the role mysticism has played in religion may seem at best irrelevant, and
at worst harmful. One only has to remember Nietzsche's stinging condemnations of
Christianity to be concerned with anything that may have helped form or shape that
religion; or, think of the numerous wars that have been fought in the name of
religion. The challenge has been ably stated as follows:

Likewise, many secular critics of the validity of mysticism such as
Freud also start from a perception of cross-cultural religious
commonality, but they take this rather as a sign of general structure
of human illusion (where not pathology) occurring at a stage of
human development outgrown with the rise of rationality and
science.[6] [emphasis added]

First, it should be noted that many actions performed in the name of religion
have been not only contrary to religious teachings and doctrine, but also seem to be
completely contrary to the mystical experience and the truths that are claimed to have
been "learned" in that experience.

Second, although mysticism has had a substantial impact on religion, it
potentially has importance for all people—including the atheist. In fact, a strong case
can be made that the Western religions of Christianity, Judaism and Islam that

4

predominantly preach belief in a personal God that can hear and answer people's prayers go well beyond the mystics' actual experiences and into an interpretive realm. This interpretation of a personal God is not seen in Buddhism, and is contrary to other Eastern religious beliefs—such as Taoism and strains of Hinduism. As such, it is not common to mystical experience in general, and the position of the atheist may well be consistent with the truly common characteristics of mystic experiences when examined cross-culturally.

It is the contention of this work that mystical experience may hold enormous import and benefit, and open up significant possibilities for all people—whether religious or otherwise. This assertion will be explored in the final chapter. For now, W.T. Stace's view on this issue may give the reader a taste of the significance of mystical experience:

> What we have to insist is that even if mystical experience is considered to be subjective it is still enormously important for human life. This refers not merely to past history, but to the future of the world. If mysticism should be treated as a mere superstition, and discouraged or exterminated—if that were possible—an immense, and indeed disastrous, disservice would be done to mankind.

> I do not consider it as any part of my function to be a preacher. But it is necessary to say here that, even if mystical experience is subjective, it is nevertheless the way of salvation. That it brings blessedness, joy, and peace is the universal testimony of those who have it whether they are religious in any conventional sense or not. And though it brings "the peace which passeth all understanding," it is not, as is often charged against it, a device of escape from the hard realities and duties of life . . . . Here it will be sufficient to say that although mysticism can be, and sometimes has been, degraded to become a mere reveling in delirious experience for its own sake, this is not of its essence, and that the greatest mystics have in fact been great workers in the world and have recognized their duty to give to the world in service what they have received in contemplation.[7]

B. The Two Central Questions Regarding Mysticism

The following shows how several notable philosophers have posed the two central questions that have driven the debate on mysticism, and should give the reader the flavor of the issues at hand.

W.T. Stace posed the questions thus:

> First, is it a fact that mystical experiences are basically the same, or similar, all over the world, or at any rate that they all have important common characteristics? Secondly, if this is true, does it constitute a good argument for believing in their objectivity?[8]

Peter Moore broached the subject as follows:

> The first line of inquiry is generally focused on the question whether the mystical experiences reported in different cultures and religious traditions are basically of the same type or whether there are significantly different types. The second line of inquiry centres on the question whether mystical experiences are purely subjective phenomena or whether they have the kind of objective validity and metaphysical significance that mystics and others claim for them.[9]

Donald Rothberg phrased his version of the questions thus:

> (1) Is there a core mystical experience, a universal experience common to humans across cultures and traditions? (2) Do mystical experiences give veridical insights into certain aspects of reality and into reality as a whole such that mystical claims should be accepted?[10]

Last, R.L. Franklin presents the inquiry in the following manner:

> (1) Is there a pure mystical experience, common to all or many traditions . . .?

> (2) If such experience occurs, what is its significance?[11]

I would like to make a few observations about these questions. First, all four philosophers show a similarity in the posing of the first question, and seem to be quite straightforward in seeking the answer to whether a common core exists among the experiences of mystics from different cultures and traditions. The second question, however, is phrased with somewhat more variation among the philosophers, and is less clear on its surface. It inquires into the objectivity, truth and/or validity of mystical claims and of the mystical experience, but gives one little guidance as to what "objectivity" in the realm of mystical experience might be. R.L. Franklin actually drops the inquiry into objectivity or truth and merely asks what is the significance of the mystical experience. This implies that the mystical experience may not be objective, but may still be significant in some other regard.

Only two of the four sets of questions imply there is a link between Question 1 and Question 2, but do not make it clear what that link may be.

What is the significance of Question 1—of determining whether there are commonalities or similarities in the mystical experiences of mystics from different times and different cultures and religions? The response to Question 1 provides some insight on how Question 2 should be answered. If there are common mystical experiences across very different traditions, this may imply that they are all tapping into the same metaphysical truths or reality—that there is something objective to the experience. If, on the other hand, the experiences of mystics are dependent on the culture or religion of the mystic, then there seems less reason to believe that the mystical experience is able to access ultimate truths or reality. In fact, if mystical experiences are radically different depending on the individual's socioeconomic-linguistic-religious background, the experience would seem to have a subjectivity that might well preclude the forcefulness of any claim to truth or other validity.

Having stated this, it should also be noted that the answer to question 1 is not necessarily determinative of the answer to Question 2. There may be a similarity or commonality throughout mystical experiences, but this does not prove that the experiences are of truth rather than illusion, as Freud pointed out. Even if there are similarities, Question 2 may be answered either that the similarities are due to human makeup and/or psychological need, or that they are due to tapping into a reality that is independent of human makeup and to that extent objective. Many people observe water in a desert even when there is no water because of a person's physical makeup that perceives the mirage as real. Likewise, the mystical experience may be "perceived" or experienced as real by many mystics, yet they all could be mistaken.

Conversely, even if there are not strong commonalities among mystical experiences, it does not dictate that some or even many of the experiences are not tapping into objective reality or metaphysical truths. For example, I may be looking at a chair and you at a table, and the fact that we both are having different experiences does not preclude the fact that we are both having an experience of an objective reality.

The significance of Question 2 seems more readily apparent. If mystics are tapping into the ultimate truths and realities that they claim, then we have much to learn from them on the issues of ethics and how we can best live our life. That humanity wishes to have guidance and certainty in these areas seems beyond doubt, but whether mysticism or anything else can provide a firm foundation is the difficult question. The mystics claim they have unlocked a reality that gives guidance on how one can and should live: living from a perspective of unity instead of multiplicity. Is this a subjective perspective that humankind has had the psychological need to invent, is it objective in that it is based on the experience of an ultimate reality, or is it something that does not fit neatly into either of these categories? These questions will later be explored.

Although the similarity among mystical experiences is not determinative of whether the mystical experience is objective and taps into metaphysical truth or reality, it is more likely that the more similar the experience among many people of many ages and traditions, the more accurate will be the reporting, understanding and interpretation of their experiences. We might well expect that many of them would have realized or concluded they were experiencing a "mirage" or an illusion if their experiences were not objective, yet such conclusions seem rare. It is for this reason that the question of similarity is relevant to the analysis of mystical experience.

It is also of significance to note that the majority of emphasis, discussion and debate by almost all Western philosophers in the last 100 years has been on the first question of commonality, and yet it is the second question to which the philosopher really seeks answers. It has been tacitly assumed by those who are skeptical about mysticism that if the mystical experiences have substantial differences, or have no common and significant similarity or core, that there can be neither metaphysical realities nor truth found in or learned from the experiences, nor even is there something worthwhile in the mystical experience. As pointed out, even without similarities, truth and value from the mystical experience are not ruled out, albeit similarities seem to make the mystic claim stronger.

Section C will look at the recent history of the philosophical debate on mysticism. Chapter 2 will look at the common characteristics of mystical experience, and Chapter 3 will examine those characteristics for potential paradoxes, inconsistencies or other problems. Chapter 4 will tackle the issues of whether mystical experience taps into objective truths or ultimate reality, and finally whether the mystic experience reveals superior perspectives or otherwise has value.

C.   History of the Recent Philosophical Debate on Mysticism

The American philosophical experts on mysticism in the first half of this century until approximately 1960 were almost uniformly convinced that there were significant similarities and commonalities among the mystical experiences of mystics from widely different cultures and eras. These philosophers, belonging to the perennial school of philosophy, believed that although the mystics characterized, described and interpreted their experiences somewhat differently owing to their different socio-religious-cultural-linguistic backgrounds, they were essentially having the same experiences. Philosophers such as William James, Evelyn Underhill and W.T. Stace were all perennialists.[12]

This view has been challenged by a view that has been labeled "constructivism," which holds that mystical experience, as all experience, is significantly shaped, determined and constructed by the mystic's beliefs, concepts and expectations. Put another way, the mystic's experience is greatly influenced by the mystic's religion, culture, language, personal habits and beliefs, and prior experiences, and the mystic cannot escape from this context.

A claim of mysticism accepted for almost 2,500 years was that one could have direct knowledge of what is ultimately real. Kant challenged this position by asserting that there is no direct, unmediated knowledge of reality, inasmuch as all human experiences are structured by human categories and human sensibilities of time and space. There is always a gap between the knower and what is known.[13]

The application of Kant's constructivism to the mystical context has been spearheaded and championed by Steven Katz in his often-cited essay "Language, Epistemology and Mysticism."[14] Katz maintains that the differences in cultures, religions, backgrounds, upbringing, etc., i.e., the context, will affect not only the interpretation of the experience, but also the experience itself. These things "mediate" the experience. As such, no two people have the same experience, and two people from widely divergent cultures and religions could not have similar experiences. The Buddhist mystic, the Sufi mystic, the Christian mystic, and the Hindu mystic will of necessity have substantially different mystical experiences. These differences are reflected in the descriptions of the mystics. It is only the Christian mystics who experience Christ in their mystic experience, and only the Buddhist mystics who experience the Buddha. The following excerpts from Katz's paper will help accurately portray his contentions and positions:

> [L]et me state the single epistemological assumption that has exercised my thinking and which has forced me to undertake the present investigation: There are No [sic] pure (i.e., unmediated) experiences.
>
> * * *
>
> A proper evaluation of this fact leads to a recognition that in order to understand mysticism it is *not* just a question of studying the reports of the mystic after the experiential event, but of acknowledging that the experience itself as well as the form in which it is reported is shaped by concepts which the mystic brings to, and which shape, his experience. To flesh this out, straight-forwardly, what is being argued is that, for example, the Hindu mystic does not have an experience of X which he then describes in the, to him, familiar language and symbols of Hinduism, but rather he has a Hindu experience, i.e., his experience is not an unmediated experience of X, but is itself the, at least partially, pre-formed anticipated Hindu experience of Brahman . . . . Moreover, as one might have anticipated, it is my view based on what evidence there is, that the Hindu experience of Brahman and the Christian experience of God are not the same . . . . The significance of these considerations is that the forms of consciousness which the mystic brings to experience set structured and limiting parameters on what the experience will be,

i.e., on what will be experienced, and rule out in advance what is "inexperienceable" in the particular given, concrete, context. Thus, for example, the nature of the Christian mystic's pre-mystical consciousness informs the mystical consciousness such that he experiences the mystic reality in terms of Jesus, the Trinity, or a personal God, etc., rather than in terms of the non-personal, non-everything, to be precise, Buddhist doctrine of nirvāna.[15]

And, I repeat, the remainder of this paper will attempt to provide the full supporting evidence and argumentation that this process of differentiation of mystical experience into the patterns and symbols of established religious communities is experiential and does not only take place in the post-experiential process of reporting and interpreting the experience itself: it is at work before, during, and after the experience.[16] [emphasis added]

One must recognize "the need to ask the fundamental question: what does the Christian bring to his experience and how does it affect that experience, and what does the Hindu bring to his experience and how does it affect that experience?"

*　　*　　*

[B]eliefs shape experience, just as experience shapes belief.[17] [emphasis added]

[I]t will not do either to argue that the empirical evidence indicates that all mystical experiences are the same or that such experiences are contextually undetermined or under-determined. The evidence we have considered to this point, in fact, points in the opposite direction: namely, mystical experience is "over-determined" by its socio-religious milieu: as a result of his process of intellectual acculturation in its broadest sense, the mystic brings to his experience a world of concepts, images, symbols and values which shape as well as colour the experience he eventually and actually has.[18] [emphasis added]

What I wish to show is only that there is a clear causal connection between the religious and social structure one brings to experience and the nature of one's actual religious experience.[19] [emphasis added]

Rather, these images, beliefs, symbols and rituals define, in advance, what the experience he wants to have, and which he then does have, will be like.[20]

> [I]t is not being argued either that mystical experiences do not
> happen, or that what they claim may not be true, only that there can
> be <u>no grounds</u> for deciding this question, i.e., <u>of showing that they are</u>
> <u>true even if they are, in fact, true</u>.[21] [emphasis added]

Katz therefore holds the following positions:

1.   Constructivism applies to the mystic experience, i.e., the mystic experience is necessarily mediated;

2.   The mystical experiences of mystics from different traditions and cultures are necessarily not similar to one another; and

3.   This lack of similarity precludes any ability to investigate or decide Question 2 regarding the truth and validity of mystical claims.

All three of the above conclusions will be challenged in this book.[22]

Katz's conclusions include his thesis of radical pluralism, which assumes that "wherever there is a difference in the conceptual scheme which the mystic brings into his experience, the mystical experience will be different."[23] As will be more fully elaborated later in Chapter 3, Katz makes two assumptions that are open to serious question:

1.   That the mystical experience cannot transcend the mystic's context; and

2.   The context will predominate over the experience to an extent that each mystical experience can rightfully be labeled as different from every other mystical experience, and should not be labeled as similar.

Although we will more thoroughly analyze and critique Katz in Chapter 3, a few points should be made here. The mystical experience, which will be elucidated in Chapter 2, is beyond the everyday experiences of our mundane world. We might call it a "limit experience" because it is fundamentally unlike ordinary experiences, therefore it is not properly subject to the same type of analysis or even logic as other experiences. As stated by J.N. Findlay, "We must not expect a limiting case to behave in the same logical manner as a case which does not fall at the limit."[24] To apply the same standards to a limit experience that we would to a normal, everyday or mundane experience is to fail to recognize the distinctions and subtleties that make the limit experience different, and the ways in which the experience pushes the "limit" of what we normally experience or even call an experience.

An example may prove instructive: Many people throughout the world report having had an out-of-body experience. Many of these experiences have occurred when a person is dying or has even been declared legally dead. Subsequently, that person has "come back to life." In these experiences, people often report seeing their bodies from an external vantage point outside their own bodies, such as from overhead. They might see themselves lying in a bed in pain, or even having been declared dead and seeing others standing over them. These people have been able to later report conversations of others that took place when their brain activity had totally ceased. If this type of experience were analyzed with the assumption that all experiences of an individual must take place with a consciousness in a live body, then the "experiences" might be called a fraud. However, to analyze the out-of-body experience as one would analyze an ordinary experience would seem to preclude the ability to properly investigate the report of the out-of-body experience. The question of whether out-of-body experiences occur would then be begged and not given its due. The out-of-body experience must be analyzed without the standard that consciousness cannot exist apart from a body, and then it can be determined if this experience is valid. Limit experiences by their nature demand that new and expanding standards be found in order to properly understand them.

In much the same way, the mystic claims the ability to "transcend oneself," to transcend space and time, and to have an unmediated experience. If one investigates mysticism with the presupposition that all experience is mediated and therefore the mystical experience is also mediated, he or she has simply begged the question and precluded a fair investigation. The limit experience must be investigated with a creative and open mind that is willing to expand and alter the standards to account for an experience that by definition is not "playing by the same rules" as ordinary experience. In much the same way, science has been able to evolve when the scientist has been willing to expand and even discard any preconceived assumptions that do not or cannot account for certain observations. Mysticism therefore, should be investigated with a mind that is both open to the claims of the mystics and is creative enough to find new standards of analysis and evaluation. This point is particularly important when examining whether the mystical experience is objective or taps into a reality that is beyond the individual and in that sense has ontological status, a topic which will be explored in Chapter 4. It may be that we need to look beyond the subjective versus objective dichotomy in order to give the mystical experience its fair due, and in order not to dismiss the mystical experience merely because by its very nature it does not and cannot conform to standards appropriate for everyday experience that do not test the "limits,"or because mystical experience lies at the edge of the normal, mundane, and common.

One more preliminary point needs to be addressed. The word "mediation" is a somewhat ambiguous term. Human experiences are normally mediated in at least three different ways:

First, our current experiences are formed and shaped by our pre-existing beliefs, ideas, memories and thoughts, and by our prior experiences that contribute to those beliefs and ideas. This would include the effect that our society, culture, religion, family and friends have on us.

Second, our experiences are mediated by our senses. We see things and thereby experience the world differently than an ant because we have different eyes, body parts and sensory apparatus. Our sensory apparatus shape our experiences.

Third, Kant pointed out that the way our minds, brains and bodies are constituted cause us to view and experience the world in specific human ways that he calls the categories of the understanding. These include categories such as quantity, quality, cause and effect, and possibility or impossibility.

The mystic claims to transcend all three types of mediation. He attempts to shut down his senses, to "forget" his past, and to become a blank slate. Moreover, the mystical experience of unity is beyond the distinctions and categories of Kant's categories of the understanding. The mystic, therefore, claims to have a truly unmediated experience.

In Chapter 2, I will explain the characteristics of a mystical experience, and attempt to illustrate the similarity in mystical experiences of persons from radically different cultures or who have lived in substantially different eras or times. Following this, in Chapter 3, the most important portion of this book, I will, among other things, expound where I think Katz is mistaken and has placed undue emphasis on the differences among mystical experiences and has either ignored or been too quick to dismiss the similarities. This will be done in the context of examining the six major philosophical criticisms of mystical claims, and the best responses that could be given by the mystic.

In Chapter 4, I will examine whether the mystical experience is purely subjective or taps into an external reality, and whether it can fairly be labeled objective. Finally, whether or not the philosophical critiques are correct, I will address the value of the mystical experience to both the individual mystic and to others, including society as a whole.

Chapter 2

The Common Characteristics of Mystical Experience

Many philosophers have attempted to provide definitions of mysticism or the mystic experience. Many of these have been rather brief and, if standing alone, would be of dubious assistance to the reader.

For example, Evelyn Underhill defines mysticism as "the art of union with Reality."[25] Gershom Scholem defined a mystic as "a man who has been favored with an immediate, and to him real, experience of the divine, of ultimate reality, or who at least strives to attain such experience."[26]

R.L. Franklin had this to say about what mysticism is:

> Mysticism is as hard to define as religion; part of the problem may be that too many diverse phenomena are collected under its name. Nevertheless, a central feature of all but borderline cases is a certain inward turning, a stilling of the ordinary activity of the mind.[27]

S.N. Dasgupta has defined the mystic quest as follows:

> I should like to define mysticism as a theory, doctrine, or view that considers reason to be incapable of discovering or of realizing the nature of ultimate truth, whatever be the nature of this ultimate truth, but at the same time believes in the certitude of some other means of arriving at it.[28]

Some definitions are more comprehensive and instructive, such as this definition offered by R.C. Zaehner:

> We have confined ourselves to praeternatural experiences in which sense perception and discursive thought are transcended in an immediate apperception of a unity or union which is apprehended as lying beyond and transcending the multiplicity of the world as we know it.[29]

Certainly, several philosophers have offered a comprehensive list of the characteristics of mysticism. W.T. Stace lists seven common characteristics of the mystical experience,[30] while Robert Gimello has set forth six such common characteristics.[31]

I have attempted to borrow from the best of these definitions and lists, and have thereupon constructed the following somewhat cumbersome definition of the mystical experience:

> A mystical experience is one in which use of the senses, reasoning and discursive thought is suspended, and there is a corresponding loss of a sense of individuality and the self. Consequently, ultimate truths and knowledge are believed to be intuitively revealed, creating an overriding sense of unity that gives a totally different perspective and outlook of one's mundane existence and the world, profoundly affecting the mystic. Even after the experience is over, the individual is transformed. He has realized an experience so different from any other that words are inadequate to convey its nature.

The reason I have posited such a comprehensive definition is to separate as much as possible the nonmystical from the mystical experience. For example, a drug experience might fall within many definitions of mysticism, but would have a difficult time meeting the criteria I have set forth since normally neither the use of the senses nor the image-making and thinking aspects of the intellect are suspended in a drug experience.

It should also be noted that some arguably mystical experiences might not satisfy all the criteria. My definition of mystical experience fails to recognize that there are different stages of the experience, and an experience that satisfies most but not all the factors may well be an early mystical stage. The definition I have set forth is meant to encompass the advanced or fully realized mystical experience. For example, the nature mystic (which Stace labels as the extrovertive mystic) does not seem to transcend or suspend the senses and has an incomplete or inchoate experience of unity, but does have enough characteristics of the mystical experience to be labeled as an early stage of mystical experience. This distinction between the extrovertive and introvertive mystic will be explained more fully.

Before explaining and providing support for my proposed common characteristics of mystical experience, which are derived directly from the definition I have proposed, a few caveats and observations are in order.

First of all, my analysis is based on texts, and texts can only go so far in accurately reflecting the mystical experience. As Katz has pointed out, the mystic must convey the experience by writing in his own language and within his own context. This point is particularly important in mysticism because we will be reading translations from other languages and from ancient times, and the accuracy of the translation into modern English is at best inexact, and at worst misleading.[32] Moreover, as an evaluator of the texts, I bring my own ideas, beliefs, concepts, culture and context.[33]

The following documentation supports what I believe to be the nine common characteristics of mystical experience. It should again be kept in mind that although I believe the evidence is quite strong regarding the similarity of many mystical experiences transculturally, this does not settle the question of whether there are ultimate truths or metaphysical or objective realities being tapped into by the mystic. This will be left for Chapter 3 to explore.

A.   Beyond Sensory Perception

The mystical experience is not obtained through the senses, such as seeing, hearing or touching. It is beyond sensory perception.

Zaehner states that "all mystics, including Ruysbroeck, agree that no progress in the inner life is possible without detachment from all things worldly, ..."[34] Dasgupta states that the "Upanishads tell us again and again that it [absolute truth] cannot be perceived by any of our senses . . . ."[35]

Evelyn Underhill, paraphrasing Blake, wrote as follows:

> If the doors of perception were cleansed, said Blake, everything

would appear to man as it is—Infinite.[36] [emphasis added]

W.T. Stace had this to say about Indian mystic experience:

> The Upanishads are of course among the earliest known documents
> of Indian mysticism, or indeed of any mysticism, dating as they do
> from the first half of the first millennium B.C. They invariably
> describe the mystical experiences as being "soundless, formless,
> intangible," i.e., devoid of sensuous content.[37]

In the Mandukya Upanishad four kinds of mental condition are delineated:
waking consciousness, dreaming, dreamless sleep and unitary consciousness.

> The fourth, say the wise . . . is not the knowledge of the senses, nor
> yet inferential knowledge. Beyond the senses, beyond the
> understanding, beyond all expression, is the fourth.[38] [emphasis
> added]

The Tao Te Ching is one of the most ancient of mystical texts, believed to
have been written by Lao Tzu, the founder of Taoism who lived at approximately the
time of Confucius (fifth and sixth centuries B.C.). Although written in paradox and
metaphor, I believe the following passage from Te Ching 19 is expressing the same
point of going beyond the sensory perceptions of the outside world.

> Block the openings,
> Shut the doors,[39]

Christian mysticism also directs one to go beyond the senses. The following
three passages are from Dionysus the Areopagite, a fifth-century Syrian monk; St.
Gregory Palamas of the Eastern Orthodox Church; and William Law, an English
post-Reformation mystic whose life spanned 1686-1762.

> . . . in the diligent exercise of mystical contemplation, leave behind
> the senses . . . .[40] [emphasis added]

> He who participates in the divine energy, himself becomes to some
> extent, light; he is united to the light, and by that light he sees in full
> awareness all that remains hidden to those who have not this grace;
> thus he transcends not only the bodily senses, but also all that can be
> known by the intellect . . . .[41] [emphasis added]

Thy natural senses cannot possess God or unite thee to Him.[42]

Meditation or contemplation has as one of its primary purposes to "shut off" sensory perceptions, and is one of the fundamental tools used by mystics throughout the world.

B. Beyond Thought

The mystical experience is beyond thought and reasoning. One must stop his image-making ability in order to go past conceptions, interpretations and beliefs, thereby establishing the freedom to have a direct and unmediated experience.

Evelyn Underhill, an early twentieth-century philosopher and mystic, beautifully states this characteristic in the following two passages:

> It is in man's moments of contact with this, when he <u>penetrates beyond all images,</u> however lovely, however significant, to that ineffable awareness which the mystics call "Naked Contemplation"— since it is <u>stripped of all the clothing with which reason and imagination</u> drape and disguise both our devils and our gods—that the hunger and thirst of the heart is satisfied, and we receive indeed an assurance of Ultimate Reality.[43] [emphasis added]

> The philosopher is a mystic when he passes beyond thought to the pure apprehension of truth.[44]

When addressing the description of a mystical experience, Dasgupta had this to say:

> It cannot be expressed in words or understood by conceptual thought; . . . We are here concerned with an experience which is non-conceptual, intuitive and ultimate.[45]

> The process of yoga consists in so controlling the activity of the mind that it ceases to pass through its different states. The cessation of all mental states is yoga.[46]

Buddhist mysticism also addresses getting beyond understanding and thought, as illustrated from this quote from *The Path of Light*: "The Reality is beyond the range of understanding."[47]

A more complete quote of one cited earlier from Dionysius the Areopagite aptly demonstrates the same point:

... in the diligent exercise of mystical contemplation, leave behind the senses and the operations of the intellect, and all things sensible and intellectual, and all things in the world of being and non-being, that thou mayest arise, by unknowing, towards the union, as far as is attainable, with Him who transcends all being and all knowledge.[48] [emphasis added]

Another Christian mystic, St. John of the Cross who lived in sixteenth-century Spain, succinctly conveyed this idea: "When thy mind dwells upon anything thou art ceasing to cast thyself upon the All."[49]

Ancient Chinese mysticism expresses the retreat from learning and understanding toward that of a quiet mind without thoughts as the path to the Way, as illustrated by these passages from the Tao Te Ching:

By not setting foot outside the door
One knows the whole world;
By not looking out the window
One knows the way of heaven.
The further one goes
The less one knows.
Hence the sage knows without having to stir,
Identifies without having to see,
Accomplishes without having to do it.[50]

Thus to understand a state through knowledge
Will be to the detriment of the state;
And to understand a state through ignorance
Will be to the good of the state.[51]

He who knows has no wide learning; he who has wide learning does not know.[52]

Exterminate learning and there will no longer be worries.
*   *   *
Mine is the mind of a fool—how blank![53]

Last, a follower of Taoism, Chuang Tzu, who lived from 369-286 B.C., expressed the quieting of the mind as follows:

The way gathers in emptiness alone. Emptiness is the fasting of the mind.[54]

C.   Loss of Self

The mystic experiences the loss of a sense of individuality, and this is most often expressed as a loss of the self. The ego, personality and individuality seem to disappear.

Stace explains this loss of a sense of self as follows:

> This is the experience of the apparent fading away, or breaking down, of the boundary walls of the finite self so that his personal identity is lost and he feels himself merged or dissolved in an infinite or universal ocean of being.[55] [emphasis added]

Underhill explains the loss of self as a loss of self-consciousness:

> When the greater love overwhelms the lesser, and your small self-consciousness is lost in the consciousness of the whole, it will be felt as an intense stillness, a quiet fruition of reality. Then, your very selfhood seems to cease, as it does in all your moments of great passion.[56] [emphasis added]

The Jewish twentieth-century mystic, Abraham Isaac Kook, described the loss of self thus:

> Then you find bliss, transcending all humiliations or anything that happens, by attaining equanimity, by becoming one with everything that happens, by reducing yourself so extremely that you nullify your individual, imaginary form, that you nullify existence in the depth of your self.[57] [emphasis added]

This loss of a sense of the self as part of the mystic experience is expressed by the three following Sufi mystics, Al-Junayd (A.D. 910), Baba Kuhi of Shiraz (died in A.D. 1050), and Jalalud-din Rumi (A.D. 1207-1273), respectively:

> The saint . . . is submerged in the ocean by unity, by passing away from himself . . . .[58]

> Myself with mine own eyes I saw most clearly, But when I looked with God's eyes -- only God I saw. I passed away into nothingness, I vanished.[59] [emphasis added]

> If thou dost desire to reach this abode of immortality, and to attain this exalted station, divest thyself first of self, and then summon unto

thyself a winged steed out of nothingness, to bear thee aloft. Clothe thyself with the garment of <u>nothingness</u> and drink the cup of <u>annihilation</u>. Cover thy breast with a nothingness, and draw over thy head the robe of <u>non-existence</u>. Set thy foot in the stirrup of complete renunciation and, looking straight before thee, ride the steed of non-being to the place where nothing is. Thou wilt be lost again and again, yet go on thy way in tranquillity, until at last thou shalt reach the world where thou art <u>lost altogether to self</u>.[60] [emphasis added]

The Chinese Taoist mystic, Chuang Tzu, cogently went to the essence of the matter: "Therefore I say, the perfect man has no self."[61]

Isvarakrsna has crystallized Indian mystic thought when he writes the following:

Thus, from the analysis of the Tattvas, arises the knowledge "I am not, nothing is mine, <u>I do not exist</u>."[62] [emphasis added]

From the *Manual of Zen Buddhism* by D.T. Suzuki, we find the following statement:

"In the higher realms of true suchness there is neither 'self' nor 'other.' "[63]

We will end our panorama regarding the loss of the self with the following excerpt from the great Christian mystic, Meister Eckhart (born in 1260):

Let us see how the soul becomes God above grace. What God has given her is changeless, for she has reached a height where she has no further need of grace. In this exalted state she has <u>lost her proper self</u> and is flowing full-flood into the unity of the divine nature.[64] [emphasis added]

D. Unity

The mystic gets in touch with "oneness" and unity. Unity predominates, envelops and even annuls the normal experience of distinct and separate entities, objects and concepts that our senses perceive and our intellects contemplate. The self is "lost" by a merging into or union with the infinite, the void, or God—arguably different labels for the same thing, as will be explored presently. Contradictories and opposites do not exist at the level of unity, but only in the diversity of the world.

There is no "me" and "you," nor "us" or "them," only a unified whole. The distinction between subject and object disappears, as does multiplicity.

There seem to be at least two different levels or degrees of unity, which Stace labels as extrovertive and introvertive. Extrovertive mysticism, which has also been called nature mysticism, sees the multiple objects and things in the world, but at the same time perceives that they are all one and form a unity. We might call this a differentiated unity. The introvertive mystical experience, on the other hand, apprehends only an undifferentiated unity, which is contentless and contains no things or objects. Stace's explanation of the difference in the two types or degrees of mysticism is instructive:

> The essential difference between them is that the extrovertive experience looks outward through the senses, while the introvertive looks inward into the mind. Both culminate in the perception of an ultimate Unity—what Plotinus called The One— with which the perceiver realizes his own union or even identity. But the extrovertive mystic, using his physical senses, perceives the multiplicity of external material objects—the sea, the sky, the houses, the trees—mystically transfigured so that the One, or the Unity, shines through them. The introvertive mystic, on the contrary, seeks by deliberately shutting off the senses, by obliterating from consciousness the entire multiplicity of sensations, images, and thoughts, to plunge into the depths of his ego. There, in that darkness and silence, he alleges that he perceives the One—and is united with it—not as a Unity seen through a multiplicity (as in the extrovertive experience), but as the wholly naked One devoid of any plurality whatever.[65]

Stace further explains the extrovertive mystical experience as follows:

> The crucial statement is that these external things, although many, were nevertheless perceived— seen by the eyes—as all one; that is, they were perceived as simultaneously many and one.[66]

Stace clarifies the introvertive mystical experience in the following manner:

> The introvertive kind of mystical states are, according to all accounts we have of them, entirely devoid of all imagery. . . . Introvertive experience is alleged by the experients of it to be void of content and formless.[67]

24

Introvertive mystical experience seems to be a more advanced stage or development of the mystical experience because it is a more complete unity that allows for no simultaneous perception of multiplicity. Extrovertive mysticism involves a unity with the material world, while introvertive mysticism involves a unity that reaches beyond the material world. Extrovertive mysticism involves use of both sensory perceptions and mental images, which are within the realm of ordinary experience, while introvertive mysticism goes beyond the purview of both the senses and the mind's images, into a world only experienced by few, and usually only after training and effort to go beyond the senses and discursive thoughts. Stace likewise believed that the introvertive type of mystical experience was a deeper, more advanced and a more important type or stage of mystical experience.

> These facts seem to suggest that the extrovertive experience, although we recognize it as a distinct type, is actually on a lower level than the introvertive type; that is to say, it is an incomplete kind of experience which finds its completion and fulfillment in the introvertive kind of experience. The extrovertive kind shows a partly realized tendency to unity which the introvertive kind completely realizes. In the introvertive type the multiplicity has been wholly obliterated. . . .[68]

> Extrovertive experience, there is some reason to think, is no more than a stepping stone to the higher introvertive state, and in any case is of less importance.[69]

Moreover, extrovertive mystical experiences often come unsolicited and unexpected, while the introvertive mystical experience of undifferentiated unity is usually acquired only through the effort of quieting the senses and the mind. As Stace notes:

> A distinction should also be made between those mystical states which have come to men unsought, without any effort on their part, and often quite unexpectedly, and those which, on the other hand, have been preceded by deliberate exercises, discipline or techniques, which have sometimes involved long periods of sustained effort. The former may be called "spontaneous," the latter—for lack of a better label—"acquired."

Spontaneous experiences are usually of the extrovertive type, though not invariably. Those which are acquired are usually introvertive, because there are special techniques of introversion—which differ only slightly and superficially in different cultures. So far as I know there are no corresponding techniques of extroversion.[70]

It should not be surprising that the introvertive mystical experience has been described as contentless since the first three criteria listed above for a mystical experience include going beyond the senses and the image-making, conception-making and reasoning intellect, and also involves loss of a sense of the self. When the mind and senses are effectively "turned off," an experience of nothingness or contentlessness, or what has been described as the "void," is what might be expected. This contentlessness transcends the normal limitations of our senses and the restrictions usually present owing to the limiting nature of the conceptions and categories in our minds, and allegedly allows for a boundless experience of the all, of the infinite, of what the Christian, Jew and Sufi interpret as God. Distinctions are not present in the contentless void, and the experience of unity or wholeness is either, arguably, what is remaining, or what I believe is more accurate, what develops as a result of the contentlessness, as will be discussed in Chapter 3, Section C. In any event, this lack of images and of boundaries is consistent with descriptions of the mystical experience as an undifferentiated unity that is both the void (nothingness) and infinite, and in the "undifferentiation" no multiplicity is possible, so only a contentless unity or wholeness remains. The apparent paradox of an emptiness that is fullness and of nothingness that is infinite is what marks the undifferentiated unity of the introvertive mystical experience, which is the experience most often reported by the mystics.

Stace explains this seeming paradox of how nothingness equates with unity as follows:

Since the experience has no content, it is often spoken of by the mystics as the Void or as nothingness, but also as the One, and as the Infinite. That there are in it no particular existences is the same as

> saying that there are no distinctions in it, or that it is an undifferentiated unity. Since there is no multiplicity in it, it is the One. And that there are no distinctions in it or outside it means that there are no boundary lines in it between anything and anything. It is therefore the boundless or the infinite.[71]

> Emptiness, the Void, Nothingness, the desert, the dark, night, the barren wilderness, the wild sea, the One—these are all equivalent expressions of the same experience of an absolute unity in which there are no empirical distinctions, ...[72]

As will be examined in Chapter 3, Section C, it is my position that the contentlessness of the mystical experience is actually an earlier stage than the profound experience of undifferentiated unity, and that the two stages have all too often been improperly conflated. On the other hand, the experience of nothingness and of the "allness" of unity are very closely related and share the common characteristics of being beyond distinctions, duality and multiplicity.

William James, who in 1902 presented his seminal work on mysticism that has provided the launching point for most of the philosophical inquiries on the subject, had this to say about the unity component of mysticism:

> The keynote of it (mystical consciousness) is invariably a reconciliation. It is as if the opposites of the world whose contradictoriness and conflict make all our difficulties and troubles, were melted into unity.[73] [emphasis added]

> We pass into mystical states from out of ordinary consciousness as from a less into a more, as from a smallness into a vastness, and at the same time as from an unrest to a rest. We feel them as reconciling, unifying states. They appeal to the yes-function more than to the no-function in us. In them the unlimited absorbs the limits and peacefully closes the account.[74] [emphasis added]

> This overcoming of all the usual barriers between the individual and the absolute is the great mystic achievement. In mystic states we both become one with the absolute and we become aware of our oneness. This is the everlasting and triumphant mystical transition, hardly altered by differences of clime or creed.[75] [emphasis added]

Dasgupta described the unity experience in the following way:

> As rivers which flow into the sea lose all their individuality in it and cannot be distinguished, so all divergent things lose their individuality and distinctions in this highest being, the ultimate reality. . . . It is, rather, a totality of partless, simple and undifferentiated experience. . . .[76]

The two famous Christian mystics, Jan Van Ruysbroeck (1293-1381) and Meister Eckhart, had this to say of the unity felt in the mystical experience:

> The God-seeing man . . . can always enter, naked and unencumbered with images, into the inmost part of his spirit. There he finds revealed an Eternal light . . . . It is undifferentiated and without distinction, and therefore it feels nothing but the unity.[77]

> The abysmal waylessness of God is so dark and so unconditioned that it swallows up within itself every Divine way and activity, and all the attributes of the Persons within the rich compass of the essential unity. . . . This is the dark silence in which all lovers lose themselves.[78]

Jewish mysticism has the notions of *Ein Sof*, which means infinite or endless, and *Ayin*, which means nothingness. The following three excerpts from these thirteenth-century Jewish mystics, Azriel of Gerona, David ben Judah he-Hasid, and Moses de Leon, demonstrate the connection between infinite and nothingness in the unity and oneness of God:

> Anything visible, and anything that can be grasped by thought, is bounded. Anything bounded is finite. Anything finite is not undifferentiated. Conversely, the boundless is call Ein Sof, Infinite. It is absolute undifferentiation in perfect, changeless oneness.[79] [emphasis added]

> Ein Sof is a place to which forgetting and oblivion pertain . . . . However, concerning Ein Sof, there is no aspect anywhere to search or probe; nothing can be known of it, for it is hidden and concealed in the mystery of absolute nothingness.[80] [emphasis added]

> Arouse yourself to contemplate, to focus thought, for God is the annihilation of all thoughts, uncontainable by any concept. Indeed,

28

since no one can contain <u>God</u> at all, it is called <u>Nothingness, Ayin</u>.[81] [emphasis added]

One expression of unity by the Sufi mystic, Gulshan-Raz, is as follows:

Every man whose heart is no longer shaken by any doubt, knows with certainty that there is no being save One . . . . In his divine majesty the <u>me</u>, the <u>we</u>, the <u>thou</u>, are not found, for the One there can be no distinction.[82]

The "ten thousand things" in Eastern thought means "all things." With this in mind, the following three quotes on unity or oneness are from the ancient Chinese Taoist Chuang Tzu:

Heaven and earth are one attribute; the ten thousand things are one horse.[83]

For this reason, whether you point to a little stalk or a great pillar, a leper or the beautiful Hsi-Shih, things ribald and shady or things grotesque and strange, the Way makes them all into one. . . . Only the man of far-reaching vision knows how to make them into one.

*   *   *

But to wear out your brain trying to make things into one without realizing that they are all the same -- this is called "Three in the morning."[84]

Heaven and earth were born at the same time I was, and the ten thousand things are <u>one</u> with me.[85] (emphasis added)

The next two excerpts regarding the unity and oneness of reality come from the eighth- and ninth-century Chinese Ch'an Buddhist masters Shi-T'an and Huang Po:

One who understands the myriad things as the self - isn't that a sage?[86]

The master said to me: All the Buddhas and all sentient beings are nothing but the One Mind, beside which nothing exists.[87]

The following two citations on oneness and unity are from the thirteenth-century Japanese Zen Buddhist masters Dogen and Daikaku:

The whole universe is one bright pearl.[88]

> You are aware of one principle pervading all the ten thousand things.
> . . . Seng-Chao says: "Heaven and earth and I are of one foot; the
> thousand things and I are one body."[89]

The contentless or emptiness of the mystical experience is indicated in the following two quotations from the ancient Chinese Tao Te Ching:

> The way is empty, ...[90]

> I attain the utmost emptiness; I keep to extreme stillness.[91]

The following two citations also address the emptiness of everything, and are from the Ch'an and Zen Buddhist masters Shih-T'ou and Ma-Tzu:

> The ultimate self is empty and void.[92]

> The Buddha is merciful and has wisdom. Knowing well the nature
> and characters of all beings, he is able to break through the net of
> beings' doubts. He has left the bondage of existence and nothingness;
> with all feelings of worldliness and holiness extinguished, [he
> perceives that] both self and dharmas are empty.[93]

Although the Tao Te Ching states that "the way is empty," the ancient Taoist Chuang Tzu again pointed out the connection between emptiness and the infinite when he stated as follows: "The Way has never known boundaries; . . . ."[94]

It is this powerful experience of Unity that most marks the mystical experience, and we will close this discussion of unity with a quote from Stace: "The Unity, the One, we shall find, is the central experience and the central concept of all mysticism. . . ."[95] As previously stated, the relationship of the mystical contentless experience and the mystical experience of unity will be further explored in Chapter 3, Section C.

E. Profound or Ultimate Truth

The mystics believe they have attained a state of "truth" and "knowing" that is beyond anything possible in the mundane world of ordinary living. It is a profound experience that reveals not only new facets of reality and truth, but also has broken through the illusions, facades and images to what is real and true.

William James characterized this aspect of the mystical experience as "noetic"—where apparent knowledge is obtained through an experience that provides "insights into depths of truth unplumbed by the discursive intellect."[96] He further explains this quality of mystical experience as follows:

> They are illuminations, revelations, full of significance and importance, all inarticulate though they remain; and as a rule they carry with them a curious sense of authority for aftertime.[97]

James seems to be describing the mystical state as one involving much greater profundity and depth than a sense experience, and one that gives access to deeper truths than can ever be arrived at by use of the intellect. The experiencers believe they have experienced "truth" in a way that neither sense perception nor intellect would give them access to, and a truth that is vitally important in the experiencer's life—more important than "truth" or knowledge arrived at by the senses or intellect.

Evelyn Underhill explains the force of the mystical experience as follows:

> This unmistakable experience has been achieved by the mystics of every religion; and when we read their statements, we know that all are speaking of the same thing. None who have had it have ever been able to doubt its validity. It has always become for them the central fact, by which all other realities must be tested and graduated.[98] [emphasis added]

Frederick Streng has listed as one of the elements of mystical experience, "The apprehension of ultimate reality, ..."[99] The ultimate reality is of the oneness or unity we have addressed.

R.C. Zaehner has the following explanation of why the mystical experience seems to tap into deeper truths and what really exists.

> In all cases the person who has the experience seems to be convinced that what he experiences, so far from being illusory, is on the contrary something far more real than what he experiences normally through the five senses or what he thinks with his finite mind. It is, at its highest, a transcending of time and space in which an infinite mode of existence is actually experienced. No wonder, then, that such an experience should appear to the subject to partake of a far greater degree of reality than our normal experiences, all of which are necessarily limited by the twin factors of space and time.[100]

St. Teresa of Avila's following statement regarding the power of the mystical experience is common among mystics from all cultures and religions:

> Anyone who has experienced this will to some extent understand. It cannot be expressed more clearly, since all that happens is so obscure. I can only say that the soul conceives itself to be near God, and that it is left with such a conviction that it cannot possibly help believing.[101]

This quote is cited here not to support St. Teresa's interpretation of her experience, i.e., that she was close to God, but rather for the conviction that the mystical experience leaves with its subject—a conviction that ultimate reality has been experienced.

F.   Different Outlook of Our World

The mystical experience of unity leaves the mystic with a radically different outlook of our everyday world. The mystic has realizations regarding the illusoriness of everyday conceptions, distinctions and experiences, believing the prior conceptions, ideas, ways of thought and modes of living to have been mistaken, misleading and limited.   The material or mundane world of existence and consciousness is often seen to be a lower plane of consciousness or existence, or a less real plane, or a plane of illusion instead of truth.   It should be noted that "illusoriness" does not necessarily mean that everyday life, ideas, experiences and objects do not exist, but rather that our conceptions of them are mistaken, misleading and limiting, i.e., things are not as we suppose them to be.

Bodhidharma, the founder of Ch'an Buddhism, set forth two separate paths or means to help one find enlightenment. The first path was "entering through the principle," and was achieved through seated wall meditation. A second path to enlightenment he called "entering through practice," which required four practices:

1.   Requiting Animosity:

This practice is based on the idea that one who is experiencing suffering is repaying a karmic debt for evil actions committed in prior lives. Once one understands that what is occurring is just and fair, acceptance of the situation will allow animosity to dissipate.

2.   Accepting Circumstances:

Once one realizes that suffering and pleasure are produced by circumstances, then one can let go of such emotions by being unmoved by circumstances.

3.   Craving Nothing:

Suffering is a result of longing and attachment. Only when one practices "craving nothing" can bliss be attained.

4.   Practice Accord with the Dharma:

This is to cultivate the understanding that there is no self, and as such, practice generosity since one needs nothing for oneself.

To really understand these four practices, a person must alter one's normal consciousness with its tendency to be concerned with the self and with blaming others and circumstances for poor fortunes. These are quite difficult and demanding practices, but lead to the realizations that seem to be common to mystical experience. Mystical experience conveys to the experiencer that personal gain, wealth, fame, and other gratifications are irrelevant and illusory. Moreover, the outside world cannot in any meaningful way adversely affect somebody who has had these mystical realizations. As such, there is no need to fight the world, and one will learn to accept what is.

Taoism likewise stresses these ideas, as the following two quotations from the Tao Te Ching and next six citations from Chuang Tzu demonstrate:

> Hence the sage desires not to desire and does not value goods that are hard to come by.[102]

> Exhibit the unadorned and embrace the uncarved block. Have little thought of self and as few desires as possible.[103]

> All were seekers of fame or gain--have you not heard of them? Even the sages cannot cope with men who are after fame or gain. . . .[104]

> So the sage harmonizes with both right and wrong. . . .[105]

He (the sage) delights in early death; he delights in old age.[106]

Resign yourself to what cannot be avoided. . . .[107]

And he who knows how to deal with circumstances will not allow things to do him harm.[108]

Men claim that Mao-Ch'iang and Lady Li were beautiful, but if fish saw them they would dive to the bottom of the stream, if birds saw them they would fly away, and if deer saw them they would break into a run. Of these four, which knows how to fix the standard of beauty for the world?[109]

Indeed, Taoism questions people's everyday standards and outlooks regarding fame, wealth, beauty, etc. A life free of desires and circumstances seems an impossible one to live for almost all people except the mystic. To harmonize with right and wrong, or life or death, to be impervious to circumstances, and to be selfless—these are abilities and outlooks that are not in our common experience.

James's following quotation of St. Teresa illustrates this characteristic well:

What empire is comparable to that of a soul who, from this sublime summit to which God has raised her, sees all the things of earth beneath her feet, and is captivated by no one of them? How ashamed she is of her former attachments. How amazed at her blindness![110]

St. John of The Cross aptly demonstrates the mystics' manner of viewing the world from a perspective of unity where selfish desires have no place.

In order to arrive at having pleasure in everything,
    Desire to have pleasure in nothing.
In order to arrive at possessing everything,
    Desire to possess nothing.
In order to arrive at being everything,
    Desire to be nothing.
In order to arrive at knowing everything,
    Desire to know nothing.[111]

Philosopher Frederick Streng explains this new outlook of unity as it applies to the mundane world in the following language:

It is so different that there is a new consciousness of purpose based on a new threshold of awareness about themselves and the world. A total awareness represents a shift in how to look at oneself and the world so that the everyday contradictions and anxieties resulting from internal or inner-outer conflicts are resolved. While conventional experience and even false perception is often reconciled within the comprehensiveness of a total consciousness, the richness of the awareness carries the mystic beyond the sense of a change in degree of awareness to the sense of a different kind of awareness.[112]

G. Deep Emotional Experience

The mystic has a deep emotional experience, often described as unsurpassable joy, peace, ecstasy, happiness and/or love; a peacefulness that is ecstasy, an overwhelming love that both calms and excites, an emptiness that is emotionally full, satisfying and enlivening. The Western mystics are the ones who often experience the stronger emotions, while the Eastern mystics normally have a more peaceful and quietly blissful mystical experience. This dichotomy will be explored later.

Philosopher R.C. Zaehner describes his own reaction to a mystical experience he had at the age of twenty:

> [T]he joy experienced as a result of this uncontrollable and inexplicable expansion of the personality is not to be brushed aside as a mere illusion. On the contrary: beside it the ordinary world of sense experience seems pathetically unreal.[113]

In this excerpt we see that the experience involved an "expansion" that led to a "joy" that was significantly more intense and real than any sensory experience.

St. Teresa of Avila likewise described the intense joy she had experienced while in a contentless mystical state:

> Here there is no sense of anything but enjoyment, without any knowledge of what is being enjoyed. The soul realizes that it is enjoying some good thing that contains all good things together, but it cannot comprehend this good thing.
>
> *   *   *
>
> While seeking God in this way, the soul is conscious that it is fainting almost completely away in a kind of swoon, with a very great calm and joy.
>
> *   *   *

> Nothing else could have robbed us of our bodily strength, yet have given us so much joy that it is returned to us increased. . . .[114]

Dasgupta, an Indian philosopher, describes the mystical experience as one of "bliss" as opposed to "joy," and again points out the contentless context in which the emotion arises:

> But when once again we are in touch with it, our so-called personality is as it were dissolved in it, and there ensues that infinitude of blissful experience in which all distinctions are lost.[115]

It is interesting that most philosophers who have listed their common characteristics of mystical experience have not included the criterion of a deep emotional experience. One who has is Robert Gimello, who uses the following language to describe the experience:

> An extraordinarily strong affective tone, again of various kinds (e.g., sublime joy, utter serenity, great fear, incomparable pleasure, etc. -- often an unusual combination of such as these).[116]

Gimello does point out that the emotion sometimes has a negative aspect to it: fear. This should not be entirely surprising since the contentless experience, or the experience of nothingness or the void, is unusual, extraordinary and unlike any other experience, and as human beings we often fear what is not known to us. Until the strength of the "unity" is experienced, the contentlessness can and has produced fear in some.

H.   Transformational

The mystical experience is tranformational. One is never the same after having a mystical experience. The mystic is able to rise above the everyday struggles, joys and hardships, and is able to obtain an equanimity that neither appreciates praise nor abhors condemnation. Having grasped or tasted the infinite and the real, the mystic's energies, attention and being are unfettered by the mundane world. The mystic finds solace and happiness in another world or dimension that he has experienced, and which leaves an indelible imprint. This does not mean that he ignores the world. Quite the contrary, the mystic, being one who lives from "a place of unity," loves and helps others. The "spiritual" truth he has experienced is brought into the everyday world. His experience of undifferentiated unity is now brought into the world as a differentiated unity.

I have listed this as a separate common characteristic of the mystical experience because a deep experience does not always transform us, an experience of new or different truths does not always cause us to think, feel and act differently, and an intense emotional experience often does not lead one to live a new and "enlightened" life.

F.C. Happold has described the transformative effect of the mystical experience thus:

> Such experiences, when they happen to a man, revolutionize his outlook, often change his life. He may carry on with his normal occupation as before. To his friends and acquaintances he may seem to be the same as he always was. But in himself he is changed. He feels that he has received a pure, direct vision of truth. Nothing can be the same again.[117]

Dante Alighieri (thirteenth-century), the great European poet, wrote these lines:

> Hence forth my vision mounted to a height
> Where speech is vanquished and must lay behind,
> And memory surrenders in such plight.
> As from a dream one may awake to find
> Its passion yet imprinted on the heart,
> Although all else is cancelled from the mind,
>   *   *   *
> That light doth so transform a man's whole bent
> That never to another sight or thought
> Would he surrender, with his own consent;....[118]
> [emphasis added]

Note that the first two paragraphs quoted above seem to indicate an experience that is beyond thought, and the final paragraph addresses its transformative nature.

This transformational aspect of the mystical experience is alluded to in Zaehner's book in which he quotes from a commentary on the Upanishad.

> Having attained to non-duality, one should behave in the world like an insensible object. The ascetic should be indifferent to praise, refrain from prayer, public worship and funeral ceremonies, he should be at home with all that moves and all that does not, and should accept whatever comes to him. Seeing the truth in respect of himself and of the external world, having himself become of the nature of truth, taking his pleasure in it, he will never depart from the truth.[119]

Evelyn Underhill probably best explains this transformative aspect of the mystical experience in the following excerpts:

> From the transitional plan of darkness, you will be reborn into another "world," another stage of realisation: and find yourself, literally, to be other than you were before.[120] [emphasis added]

> But this experience, this "ascent to the Nought" changes for ever the proportions of the life that once has known it; gives to it depth and height, and prepares the way for those further experiences, that great transfiguration of existence which comes when the personal activity of the finite will gives place to the great and compelling action of another power.[121] [emphasis added]

> Living in this atmosphere of Reality, you will, in fact, yourself become more real . . . if you practice with diligence the arts which I have described: then, sooner or later, you will inevitably find yourself deeply and permanently changed by them -- will perceive that you have become a "new man." Not merely have you acquired new powers of perception and new ideas of Reality; but a quiet and complete transformation, ...[122] [emphasis added]

I.   Ineffability

James states that a mystical experience is ineffable because it "defies expression, that no adequate report of it can be given in words."[123] This definition indicates that not only have we not yet developed adequate words to describe the mystical state, but rather, there is something about the mystical experience that militates against a word description. The ineffability is more than the difficulty one would have in describing a sense experience, such as describing hearing to one who is deaf. The experience is a "difference in kind" from all other experiences where verbal or written descriptions are much more helpful and accurate. It is not an

38

experience of a material or tangible object as is true of sensory experiences. The reasons for such ineffability will be discussed in the next chapter.

The characteristic of ineffability is a common theme in the Tao Te Ching. The Tao Te Ching, and Chinese thought in general, address the concept of "The Way," an elusive concept at best. "The Way" seems to be similar to the ultimate truths of the contentless mystical experience in that it is characterized as infinite, invisible, unchanging, forever, and indescribable. It is truth, which is constant and beyond time and space. This ineffability is demonstrated by the following three passages in the Tao Te Ching:

> The way can be spoken of, but it will not be the constant way.[124]

> The way is constantly nameless.[125]

> One who knows does not say it; one who says it does not know it.[126]

Pai-Chang, a Ch'an Buddhist master who lived in China from A.D. 720-814, talked of the sage, who is an enlightened person and lives according to the Way, as follows:

> The substance of the sage is nameless and cannot be spoken of.[127]

In speaking of the unity or "one mind" of all sentient beings, this mystical or transcendent unity and its impossibility of description was stated well by master Huang-Po (circa A.D. 840):

> It is neither long nor short, big nor small, for it transcends all limits, measures, names, traces, and comparisons. It is that which you see before you—begin to reason about it and you at once fall into error.[128] [emphasis added]

This belief that words cannot describe the Way, cannot describe what is beyond common experience and is mystical, is put succinctly by Lin-Chi (circa A.D. 860s): "Followers of the Way, don't search for anything in written words."[129]

In Christian mysticism, the contentless experience of undifferentiated unity is interpreted as God, and not surprisingly, the Christian mystics have an inability to describe God, unlike their religious nonmystical counterparts.

For example, Dionysius the Areopagite, had this to say about God:

> Again, ascending yet higher, we maintain that He is neither soul nor intellect; nor has he imagination, opinion, reason or understanding; nor can He be expressed or conceived,. . . His absolute nature is outside of every negation -- free from every limitation and beyond them all.[130] [emphasis added]

Meister Eckhart, in Tractate II, had a similar idea about the inexpressibility of the mystical experience of God:

> God is not light nor life nor love nor nature nor spirit nor semblance nor anything we can put into words.[131] [emphasis added]

J.   Excluded Characteristics

Four other possible common characteristics of the mystical experience have been included in some philosophers' lists, but I have chosen not to include them in mine: transience, passivity, the transcendence of time and space, and paradoxicality.

William James included transiency and passivity as two of his four marks of the mystical experience. He explained what he meant by transiency as follows:

> Mystical states cannot be sustained for long. Except in rare instances, half an hour, or at most an hour or two, seems to be the limit beyond which they fade into the light of common day. Often, when failed, their quality can but imperfectly be reproduced in memory; but when they recur it is recognized; and from one recurrence to another it is susceptible of continuous development in what is felt as inner richness and importance.[132]

My first reaction to this characteristic is that it is trivially true because all experiences are by their nature transient. Our experiences are ever-changing as our consciousness on and attention to matters change. No experience lasts very long, and more important, all experiences must give way to new experiences. To label mystical experiences as transient seems to tell us almost nothing of substance about the experience.

Second, to the extent that an experience could be called transient in that once it is over it may have little effect or "staying power" in our lives, this seems to be the opposite of the mystical experience, which affects the subject profoundly and transformatively. In Zen Buddhism, once enlightenment is achieved, it seems that it is often able to be maintained. In Zen Buddhism, enlightenment is to be transferred from master to student, but if the enlightenment experience were so transient as to be only a dim memory once it was over, there would appear to be little that the master could teach the student, i.e., it would seem to be difficult to transmit what one cannot maintain oneself.

Indeed, the mystical experience would apparently be no more transient than other experiences, and if anything, it is more present and conscious in the mystic's mind and consciousness than would be the case following most other experiences.

William James clarifies what he means by "passivity" with the following remarks:

> Although the oncoming of mystical states may be facilitated by preliminary voluntary operations, as fixing the attention, or going through certain bodily performances, or in other ways which manuals of mysticism prescribe; yet when the characteristic sort of consciousness has set in, the mystic feels as if his own will were in abeyance, and indeed sometimes as if he were grasped and held by a superior power.[133]

I have mixed feelings about this criterion, as it seems James himself did. First of all, James has made it clear that the mystic experience is often initiated by purposeful activities, and as such it seems somewhat misleading to call the experience passive. Second, many experiences have a passive element. For example, when we eat, we consciously act to feed ourselves, but thereafter may "passively" enjoy the tasting experience. Third, the description of being "grasped and held by a superior power" would appear much more applicable to the Western world mystics and inapplicable to the Eastern mystics, many of whom neither experience nor believe in God, nor feel themselves to be directed by another power.

In view of the above, I find the listing of passivity to be somewhat misleading and of marginal instructive or analytic value.

A third characteristic that I have not included but is sometimes listed as common in the mystical experience is that of the transcendence of time and space. Stace calls this being nonspatial and nontemporal,[134] and Zaehner makes the strong claim that "nature mysticism means to transcend space and time."[135]

I would first like to point out that many mystical accounts make no mention of the transcendence of space and time, although it arguably can be inferred from the nature of the experience. To the extent it is present, I believe it is a part of both the "unity" characteristic and the "loss of sense of self" characteristic. When one has no sense of self, consciousness of time and space are not present. Moreover, from the perspective of unity and wholeness, the multiplicity inherent in time and space cannot be seen or experienced. Stace himself recognizes that this characteristic is really inherent in undifferentiated unity when he explains a quotation of Eckhart as follows:

> We see in this quotation a further implication of the experience of the undifferentiated unity. It must necessarily be spaceless and timeless, because space and time are the very conditions and exemplars of multiplicity.[136]

The last possible common characteristic of the mystical experience to be considered is paradoxicality. This is one of Stace's common characteristics, and is included in the list of Robert Gimello's common characteristics in the following words: "A sense of the coincidence of opposites, of various kinds (paradoxicality)."[137]

Paradox is often found in the accounts of the mystical experience. It is used in at least two very distinct ways, however, descriptively and instructively. When it is used to describe the mystical experience, the paradox is a symptom or result of the ineffability of the mystical experience, and I have therefore not included this as a separate criterion. More will be said on descriptive paradox in the next chapter.

Paradox is quite commonly used, moreover, especially by the Eastern mystics, as a tool to help facilitate students down the path toward mystical experience. There are many techniques used to attempt to slow the mind to allow for the contentless mystical experience. One of these is contemplation or meditation, of which there are innumerable methods and techniques. Another method is the use of paradox because if contrary statements are truly inconsistent and irreconcilable, but are to be considered as a whole, contemplation on their overall meaninglessness can assist the student/seeker in overcoming his or her normal reasoning and discursive thought. In order to have a mystical experience, the subject must go beyond normal consciousness and thinking, and paradox is one tool to facilitate one's crossing from the world of ordinary experience to the mystical.

This recognition of paradox and of seemingly inconsistent or meaningless language as having instructive value and not always a descriptive function has been noted by several philosophers. For example, Frits Staal, in his 1975 paper titled "The Alleged Irrationality of Mysticism," pointed out that seeming irrational and meaningless expressions, such as the Indian mantra, were not to be taken literally but rather were to be considered as aids in meditation and in altering mental states to be conducive for mystical experience.

> The reason is that one feature of such apparently irrational statements is that they are not statements at all, but instruments of therapy, intended to bring about a change in mental state.[138]

> The main function of such mantras, however, has nothing to do with the expressive function of a natural language. They are instruments bringing about a change in mental state and are used, for example, as aids in meditation. To insist that mantras are irrationalistic is therefore to miss the point. And what holds for mantras holds for many other religious statements. The therapeutic value of such statements does not support irrationalism.[139]

Frederick Streng has also recognized that paradox and other seemingly irrational mystical language often have an instructive or transformative function instead of a descriptive function.

> Another function of language found in mystical language is just as important. It is to evoke a change in attitudes and mechanisms of apprehension within the mystic adept, as exemplified in some of the mystical expression of Indian Mahayana Buddhist literature.[140]

To summarize this point, when paradox is used as an instructive tool, it is not a characteristic of the mystical experience itself, and when it is descriptive in nature, it would seem to fall within the ineffability characteristic.

Indeed, I believe there is strong evidence of a striking similarity in mystical experiences across different cultures and time periods, yet this does not mean we should not pay attention to the differences. In spite of the similarities, several important questions remain. First, is the mystical experience as described by the mystics internally inconsistent or paradoxical in a way that we should doubt its rationality and claims? This will be explored in the next chapter.

Second, do the mystics tap into either an ultimate truth or other realities and truths that have any objectivity to them? Third, if the second question is either unanswerable or should be answered "no," is there significant value to the mystical experience in any event? These questions will be discussed in Chapter 3.

Chapter 3

Six Philosophical Attacks on Mystical Claims

Many philosophers and religious leaders have been skeptical about mystical claims. Mystical claims often challenge religious doctrine and the often-seen assertion of a religion that its views are the only one that conform to reality and truth. The philosopher, on the other hand, might well say that even if there are similarities in mystical experiences cross-culturally, the conclusions and claims of the mystics drawn from their experiences are internally inconsistent, paradoxical, contradictory, contrary to the way the world actually is, insulting to common sense, and irrational.

The distrust of mysticism in the West has been well put by Frits Staal:

> [R]ationalism and religion have in the West become opposite and competing trends. Since mysticism is generally, though I think erroneously, regarded as part of religion (despite the uneasiness most mystics have felt in the Christian and Muslim traditions), there is therefore a widespread prejudice that mysticism too is not susceptible to rational, objective analysis.[141]

Staal concludes that most reports of mystical experience are not irrational, and that in fact many mystics, especially the more philosophical mystics, rely on rationality, unlike many Christian theologians who rely on faith over rationality.

> Let us return to Christianity. Many Christian theologians defend Christianity not only because it emphasizes the irrational but also the personal, the historical, and the unique; and they reject mysticism because of its emphasis not only on rationality, but also on what is impersonal, eternal, and general. In Christianity, God has become man only once, God has created the world out of nothing only once, and man lives only once (see e.g., Cullman 1968; Puech 1951, and the references listed there). But in many forms of mysticism, uniqueness is rejected in favor of repeatability, commonality, and generality, just as the personality of God is often rejected in favor of an all-pervading

46

impersonal divine absolute.[142]

Staal closes his article with the following remarks:

> All these considerations show that many of the claims contained in
> mystical doctrines, whether true or false, are not only not irrational,
> but that their rationality is similar in structure to that of the sciences.
> I do not claim that this is something that makes mysticism more
> respectable or for which it is necessarily to be commended. Nor does
> it establish that mysticism is rational. But it shows that mysticism
> and rationality are compatible, and it indicates that it is entirely
> erroneous to suppose that mysticism cannot be studied at all.[143]

With the foregoing in mind, I would like to examine six areas in which
critics might find irreconcilable paradox, inconsistency, claims contrary to fact,
claims violative of common sense, or other troubling concerns. It is my intention to
illustrate Staal's conclusion to be correct: that mysticism and rationality not only can
be and are consistent with each other, but are complementary to each other as well.
Again, we should keep in mind that rationality and consistency do not in and of
themselves validate the truth of mystical claims; however, those claims should be
given their due consideration without any presumption of their falsehood or
inconsistency with our modern scientific world view.

A.   **Challenge 1: Ineffability**

Virtually all of the mystics claim that their experience is ineffable and beyond
the realm of description, yet so many mystics write voluminously, articulately,
practically and lucidly about their experience. They in fact describe what they claim
is the indescribable. Peter Moore has succinctly stated the question as follows:
"[W]hy, if mystical experience is ineffable, do mystics write so much about it?"[144]

That a person would attempt to describe a profound experience that is unlike
any other experience should not be too surprising. The mystic would claim that the
profundity compels him to try to give to others a glimpse into or a "flavor" of the
deepest experience of his life. The experience of unity often brings with it an
overwhelming love of one's fellow man, so it is not surprising that the mystic would

wish to share his experience and encourage others to seek the experience.

The question remains, however, as to whether the mystics have correctly labeled the experience as ineffable. Is there something about the experience that makes words inadequate in a sense that is beyond the normal difficulty of describing any experience? I think the answer is "yes" from several perspectives, but before we explore this we should complete the challenge to any claim of ineffability. Some skeptics about the mystical experience, as demonstrated in the quotation from Katz below, do not claim that mystics merely mislabel their experiences as ineffable, but seem to inject a sinister purpose into the ineffability claim—the purpose of precluding investigation into mystical claims altogether.

> [T]he terms "paradox" and "ineffable" do not function as terms that inform us about the content of experience, or any given ontological "state of affairs." Rather they function to cloak experience from investigation and to hold mysterious whatever ontological commitments one has. As a consequence, the use of the terms "paradox" and "ineffable" do not provide data for comparability, rather they eliminate the logical possibility of the comparability of experience altogether.[145] [emphasis added]

Of course, the fact that so many mystics do their best to describe the mystical experience takes some thunder away from Katz's charge that mystics hide behind their ineffability claim. The fact is, mystics do the best they can in describing their experiences, but uniformly feel that their descriptions fall far short of adequately conveying what was actually experienced. Why do they so uniformly feel this sense of failure?

I would like to answer this question in two ways, but which I think are really "two sides of the same coin." The first explanation would be more in conformity with the Western mystics and the belief in an infinite God, while the second explanation is somewhat more Eastern in approach and stresses nothingness over infinity.

Let us recall that the undifferentiated unity of the unitive contentless experience is in one regard an experience or taste of infinity—it is the wholeness that includes the all or infinite and from which *no* diversity, duality or multiplicity can be seen or experienced. The unitive contentless experience is one without conceptual or mental boundaries, and in that respect is infinite and attains complete freedom. But we, as finite human beings using finite language, cannot possibly explain the infinite. By definition, finite terms and categories cannot capture the infinite. From a logical standpoint, the finite cannot accurately portray the infinite; they are differences in kind, not merely differences in degree.

The reason I have categorized this explanation as being Western in nature is because it focuses on the infinite, which is one of the primary ways in which God is defined. The Christian mystic, Nicholas de Cusa, expressed this inability of the finite human intellect to grasp the infinite, and if the infinite cannot be properly grasped it certainly cannot be adequately expressed.

> How can the intellect grasp Thee, who art infinity? The intellect knoweth that it is ignorant, and that Thou canst not be grasped because Thou art infinity. For to understand infinity is to comprehend the incomprehensible.[146]

The thirteenth-century Jewish mystic Azriel of Gerona also expressed the incompatibility of the finite mind with the infinite undifferentiated unity.

> Anything visible, and anything that can be grasped by thought, is bounded. Anything bounded is finite. Anything finite is not undifferentiated. Conversely, the boundless is called Ein Sof, Infinite. It is absolute undifferentiation in perfect, changeless oneness.[147]

On the other side of the coin, the undifferentiated unity is not only infinite, it is also nothingness in that no separate entity or things are or can be experienced. There are no conceptions or differentiations present. But language, by its very nature, categorizes, conceptualizes, compartmentalizes, differentiates and limits. Words all have limits and differentiate one concept or idea from another. As such, words and language can at best attempt to conceptualize what is beyond any conceptions. It is a logical impossibility to adequately conceptualize and differentiate what is unconceptualizable and undifferentiated, and as such, the mystical experience is truly ineffable.

Frederick Streng has explained this perspective of ineffability as follows:

> The attempt to conceptualize and articulate the mystical awareness results in paradoxes because two irreconcilable notions are juxtaposed: an undifferentiated whole and undifferentiated concepts and images interrelated through classificatory schemes and a principle of non-contradiction.[148]

In the undifferentiated unity, there is a loss of the self so that no duality is experienced. The unity transcends our normal subject-object manner of experiencing the world, and only unity remains. According to Gershom Scholem, the late expert on Jewish mysticism, our language presupposes a subject-object relationship that does not exist in the mystical experience.

> In itself it has no adequate expression; mystical experience is fundamentally amorphous. The more intensely and profoundly the contact with God is experienced, the less susceptible it is of objective definition, for by its very nature it transcends the categories of subject and object which every definition presupposes.[149] [emphasis added]

Stace does a masterful job of explaining the ineffability of the mystical experience, pointing out that concepts and words live in the world of multiplicity, while the mystical experience resides in a world of unity.

> The theories which we are to examine in this section seek to explain ineffability as being due to an incapacity of the understanding or intellect to deal with mystical experience. The usual account of the matter asserts that mystical experience is inherently incapable of being conceptualized. It can be directly experienced, this theory states, but it cannot be abstracted in concepts. But since every word in language, except proper names, stands for a concept, it follows that where no concepts are possible no words are possible. Therefore mystical experiences being uncon-ceptualizable are also unverbalizable. For this reason ineffability is not a matter of degree, as for example the emotion theory supposes, but is absolute and ineradicable. Such is the common theory. [emphasis added]
>
> The theory should explain why mystical experience is unconceptualizable. In the case of introvertive experience, the reason might be that it is an undifferentiated unity, empty of all empirical

content, formless and void. There are in it no distinguishable items. But concepts depend on there being a multiplicity of distinguishable items. The mind notes resemblances and differences between them and arranges those which resemble each other in certain ways into the same class. The idea of the class is the concept. Hence where there is no multiplicity there can be no concept and therefore no words. [emphasis added]

*　　*　　*

The essential point is here clearly made that concepts depend on multiplicity and can therefore find no foothold in an experience which is wholly unitary.

*　　*　　*

It is the formlessness, the lack of any definite shape, which is here said to make the experience ineffable. Since the experience is the empty void, without specifiable content, there are no definite forms on which the concept can fix. The formless is the same as the empty or void. It is 'not this, not that.' And since every concept or word stands for a this as distinguished from a that, no concepts or words are possible. Thus Eckhart also supports the theory of unconceptualizability.[150] [emphasis added]

Robert Forman has a very different, but equally convincing way of explaining why the mystical experience is inherently ineffable. To oversimplify his position, which is stated below, words are contentful and the mystical experience is contentless, or as he states, the mystical experience by its very nature demands that language be transcended or forgotten, and hence the difficulty of later using language to describe an experience where the lack of language is crucial. PCE refers to the Pure Consciousness Event, which is the contentless mystical experience.

This model also accounts nicely for the well-known ineffability of mystical experiences. In general: What makes me able to speak of something without feeling that "words are inadequate?" When I look at the shiny, brass, cylindrical object near the edge of the door in front of me, the word "doorknob" comes readily to mind. It is not a later addition to my wordless experience of the cylindrical object, it is part and parcel of my experience. To see a doorknob is to think -- consciously or very nearly so -- the word "doorknob." Were I to report on that experience, I would say that I saw or turned a doorknob. The language I use to express the experience would include the very term I had employed in the original experience (or something very near to it). This is why my report seems to 'fit' my experience. The language of the experience is the same as the report. Logically, there is a necessary connection between descriptive language and the language of the primary experience. Change the language of the experience -- "Oh that's not a doorknob, it's a cardboard model!" -- and the language of the report must change.

Similarly, when I tell my friend of an insight I had, I do so using just the language -- or something very near to -- the very words which I originally thought. Again the language of the secondary report may be (and probably is) just the same or very similar to the language used in the primary experience.

According to the forgotten model, however, during the PCE, language, *all* language, is forgotten. Therefore, any language used to describe or report on that experience is *not* language which was employed in the primary event. There *can* be no identity of language between the primary experience and the report: there *must* be a disjunction. Logically, there is only a *contingent* connection between descriptive language and the primary experience. It is to this intuition of a linguistic disjunction that the mystic correctly avers with the term "ineffable."[151]

Indeed, what we have found is that the ineffability of mystical experience is neither an attempt to preclude inquiry into the mystical experience or mystical claims, nor is it the normal difficulty present in describing any experience. Rather, it is more on the order of a logical difficulty of having finite language express an experience of the infinite, or alternatively having a contentless and undifferentiated experience portrayed by contentful and differentiated language and words. Yet, these difficulties do not make the mystical experience invalid, inconsistent or contradictory, as is enunciated in this quotation from Frits Staal:

> [T]here is nothing irrational about the *catuskoti*, and that it merely expresses the inapplicability of ordinary language to absolute reality:
>
> * * *
>
> But the view that there are realms of reality where ordinary language is not applicable is not, of course, paradoxical, inconsistent, or contradictory. Such a situation is quite common not only in philosophy but also elsewhere, e.g., in mathematics or engineering, where for that reason artificial languages are constructed. Whenever

we have semantically ill-formed expressions, the same situation obtains; for example, it does not make literal sense to say that grass is intelligent, or that it is not. In such cases, where neither A nor not A is applicable, the principle of the excluded middle does not hold.[152]

Now that we have seen why the mystical experience is truly ineffable, i.e., cannot adequately be conveyed in words, we may wish to again visit the question of how so much can be written about such an inexpressible experience. Are the words merely symbolic and not to be taken literally? I think the answer to the question is that many of the descriptions are more than symbolic—they are the best possible attempts to explain what literally occurred during the experience. As to the emotions experienced, there is no insurmountable difficulty, but as we have seen regarding the contentless experience or the experience of undifferentiated unity, a Herculean challenge remains for the mystic. Usually, he or she can do little more than compare the experience to other mundane experiences, often explaining where a difference lies.

Below are two fairly extensive quotations that explain why the mystics can write so much about an inherently inexpressible experience. The first, written by Prigge and Kessler, explains that positive descriptions can be made about the context of the experience, but that only negative descriptions can be made of the experience itself inasmuch as it is contentless.

> If we define pure consciousness as contentless consciousness, the problem of ineffability can be handled easily. One can talk about an experience either by describing what is intrinsic to it or by describing some aspect of its context. But since a unitive mystical experience neither is, nor has a content of, consciousness, no content whatsoever is intrinsic to it; in this sense it is ineffable. On the other hand, a unitive mystical experience, like any other experience, has a context, and to the extent the context can be described, to that extent the experience can be talked about. Hence, one cannot say of a unitive mystical experience what it was of, who was sensed in the experience as having it, or what simpler experiences made it up. One can say, of course, who had the experience, when and where he or she had it, and so forth, all these latter matters having to do with the context of the experience. One can also say that the experience had no object, no

(sensed) subject, no simpler experiential parts, in short, that it was contentless, that nothing was intrinsic to it, and, in that sense, that nothing can be said about it. Such "descriptions" may be generalized, as herein, so as to apply to all such experiences. But these "descriptions" adhere strictly to the *via negativa*: they say what the experience is not, not what it is. Any positive description of a particular pure consciousness or of all such experiences in general will either be itself a genuine, though not readily obvious, negation, as is the case with the characterization of the unitive mystical experience as being tranquil or eternal -- or else it will be an affirmation about some aspect of its context -- as is the case with the characterization of the unitive mystical experience as bringing tranquility, or knowledge, or whatever. Therewith is resolved the paradox of saying so much about what one says one can say nothing about.[153] [emphasis added]

The second quotation, with which this discussion on ineffability will end, is by Stace and points out that although conceptions and words are inapplicable during the experience, once the mystical experience is over, the mystic is free to use his conception-making ability to explain the experience. In other words, once the mystic is back in the world of multiplicity, he can use language that depends on that same multiplicity to describe the unitive mystical experience, though the ineffability remains, i.e., the descriptions are both helpful and inadequate in a very fundamental way.

> Mystical experience, *during* the experience, is wholly unconceptualizable and therefore wholly unspeakable. This *must* be so. You cannot have a concept of anything *within* the undifferentiated unity because there are no separate items to be conceptualized. Concepts are only possible where there is a multiplicity or at least a duality. Within a multiplicity, groups of similar items can be formed into classes and distinguished from other groups. We then have concepts and therefore words. Within the undifferentiated unity there is no multiplicity, and therefore there can be no classes, no concepts, and no words. We cannot, for example, *at that time* class it and speak of it as "undifferentiated," for this is to classify it as distinct from what is differentiated. We cannot speak of it as "unity" or the "One" because to do so is to distinguish it from multiplicity.

But afterwards when the experience is remembered the matter is quite different. For we are then in our ordinary sensory-intellectual consciousness. We can contrast the two kinds of consciousness. Our experiences can be seen to fall into two classes, those which are differentiated and multiple and those which are undifferentiated and onefold. Since we now have concepts, we can use words. We can *speak* of an experience as "undifferentiated," as "unity," as "mystical," as "empty," as "void," and so on.

The result of confusing these two quite different situations has been disastrous. It has led to the theory that even a remembered mystical experience cannot be spoken of except in symbolic language. *Theorists have supposed that the impossibility of using concepts during the experience is also characteristic of the remembered experience.* Hence even the experience in memory has been supposed to be unconceptualizable and unutterable. But, since mystics do in fact use words about it, it has been wrongly supposed that they can only be symbolic.[154] [emphasis added]

B.   Challenge 2: Contentlessness

Let us recall Katz's acknowledged assumption that there are no unmediated experiences.

To get a clearer conception of what this paper is after when it speaks of the issue of 'Why mystical experiences are the experiences they are,' let me state the single epistemological assumption that has exercised my thinking and which has forced me to undertake the present investigation: *There are No pure (i.e. unmediated) experiences.* Neither mystical experience nor more ordinary forms of experience give any indication, or any grounds for believing, that they are unmediated. That is to say, *all* experience is processed through, organized by, and makes itself available to us in extremely complex epistemological ways. The notion of unmediated experience seems, if not self-contradictory, at best empty.[155]

I believe Katz's assumption about experience always being mediated contains an even more fundamental presumption, namely, that all experience has content, or, expressed negatively, that no experience is contentless. Since it would seem that a contentless experience could not possibly be mediated since there is nothing to mediate, Katz must assume that the contentless experience as described by the mystics is impossible. Katz has really made the following two arguments:

First Argument:

1.   All experiences have content;

2.   All contentful experiences are mediated;

3.   Therefore, all experiences are mediated.

It should be noted that premises #1 and #2 are both assumptions, and that the mystics' reports of a contentless experience directly challenge premise #1. While premise #2 may be true for ordinary experience, it may be inapplicable to the mystical experience of unity.

Second Argument:

1.   All mediated experiences are different;

2.   Therefore all mystical experiences are different;

3.   Due to these differences, most if not all mystical experiences are either not getting in touch with a common, objective reality, or it is at least impossible to know if they are.

This second argument will be examined more thoroughly in Chapter 3, Section D, but for now, we should note that to say that all mediated experiences are different is not to say that they are not substantially similar, and likewise to claim that all mystical experiences are different is not to demonstrate that they are not similar. Moreover, substantial similarity does provide some verification and support to mystical claims.

I believe that Katz's epistemological assumption that all experiences are mediated and his resulting conclusion that the experiences are therefore different so as to make mystical claims inherently unverifiable is open to serious doubt. My position is as follows:

First, there are good reasons for believing that many mystical experiences are contentless and unmediated;

Second, even if all mystical experiences have a small amount of content and a small amount of mediation, this would not be enough to mandate a conclusion of substantial differences in experience nor a claim of total insubstantiation of mystical claims.

Let us first examine what good reasons there are for believing many mystical experiences are contentless and unmediated. There are two areas of support for this claim:

1.   Mystical reports and accounts that claim their experience was contentless; and

2.   Medical evidence that mental and physical activity are substantially reduced while in the mystical state.

We have already cited many mystics who have claimed to have had the contentless mystical experience. Indian Buddhists call this experience the attainment of cessation, or the cessation of sensation and conceptualization.[156] Christian mystics have referred to the experience as a barren desert, darkness, and silence. Jewish mystics have their concept of *Ayin* or nothingness. The Upanishads talk of a state in which the five senses, thought, intellect and mind all cease to operate, and call this "Yoga."[157] The Buddhist concept of Nirvana is the state of "absolute extinction of the mind" and the cessation of all sorrows and suffering.[158] Meister Eckhart used the term "gezucken" to describe a pure consciousness event where the mind was "simultaneously wakeful and devoid of content for consciousness."[159] "Sunyata" is the term for the Buddhist Void or emptiness.[160]

Moreover, contentless consciousness is actively sought in many mystical traditions, and contemplation and meditation are performed specifically with this purpose in mind.

The following quotation from philosopher Donald Rothberg sums up quite nicely the weakness of Katz's assumption that there are no contentless, unmediated experiences:

> Is there a reading of the evidence from mystical traditions rendering, at least, plausible counter theses to Katz's thesis that all experience is mediated? There are, I find, at least two kinds of possible countertheses possible on alternative readings of mystical traditions.

The first— supported by the analysis of the reports of many mystics that show no clear signs of mediation—is that some experiences are not mediated, are not constructions rooted in religious traditions. The second—suggested by the practices of many mystics—is that there is an important class of spiritual practices designed to recognize, work with, and overcome in significant ways the mediated or constructed quality of human experience. The experiences of mystics seem to suggest that these practices are effective. Hence, in a very significant way, many forms of mysticism do not represent—against the claims of Katz and others—simply forms of reconditioning; arguably, they involve substantial deconditioning.

On the first point—that some experiences are not constructed—it is clear that many mystics claim that they experience a transcendence of the various forms of mediation. Phenomenologically, this experience is described positively as one of pure consciousness or undifferentiated unity, and it is described more negatively as an experience of the unconditioned. One main task of the present work is to argue that humans can at times be wakeful but in a way devoid of content and intentionality and that this way of experiencing is central to many mystical traditions.[161]

In addition to the testimony of many mystics across radically different cultures, religions and traditions that they have achieved a consciousness and awareness without content and intentionality (i.e., of an object), medical evidence suggests that mystical techniques can substantially slow down or even stop major aspects of the functioning of the body and mind.

Roland Fischer has put forward a "cartography" of conscious states that includes all mystical states. The quiet mystical states, such as yoga samadhi, show an incredibly low heart rate, skin temperature, spontaneous galvanic skin responses and electroencephalogram (EEG) patterns.[162] The EEG, which measures brain activity, has been measured to be radically reduced while in a deep meditative state. Studies by J.T. Farrow and J.R. Hebert have even found a stoppage of breathing for prolonged periods while one is in a meditational state.[163]

Moreover, studies have given some indication that focusing on only one object can "shut down" the ability to perceive. For example, "Newton was the first

58

to note that when a retinal image is stabilized it tends to disappear."[164] Troxler noted that if one steadily fixates on patches of color, the colors tend to fade. This phenomenon has been verified in many studies and is called the "Troxler effect."[165]

Additionally, there is evidence that continuous uniform stimulation can cause imagelessness in consciousness. This is described by Forman as follows:

> The effect with the closest parallel to mystical "forgetting" may be the one that is produced when an observer is placed in a so-called *Ganzfeld*, a completely patternless visual field. A whitewashed surface or a blizzard can serve as a Ganzfeld, as can two halves of a Ping-Pong ball taped over the eyes. At first, observers may see the whiteness as a fog or cloud; within several minutes, things seemed to go black. Some experimental Ganzfeld subjects even thought that someone turned the lights off. After a while (ten to twenty minutes), observers frequently reported what they called "blackout." This was not merely the experience of seeing nothing but that of not seeing, a complete disappearance of the sense of vision for short periods . . . . During the blackout, the observers did not know, for instance, whether their eyes were open or not, and they could not even control their eye movements . . . . [C]ontinuous uniform stimulation resulted in the failure of any kind of image to be produced in consciousness.[166]

Forman then compares these results to the meditational and other mystical techniques that are used in order to achieve the contentless consciousness:

> Under conditions of steady or regular sensory input, in other words, senses and sensations are commonly forgotten.
>
> Turning to mystical techniques, Ornstein and Naranjo and Piggins and Morgan have suggested that the common meditative practices of restricting awareness to a single unchanging process may be analogous, since both involve a great deal of repetition. They point out that the object of one's attention may be in any sense modality: verbal-like mantras, dervish calls, or short prayers; visual (a *yantra* candle or guru's picture); or the concentration may be on a regular bodily process like the heartbeat or the breath. What seems critical is that the procedure typically incorporates repetition of a "mental subroutine."[167]

Indeed, what these studies indicate is that simple repetitions seem to be able to slow or even stop the body and mind's normal functioning, and these findings lend support to the mystics' claims of having a contentless experience which involves shutting down the mind to everyday external influences and internal thought. This lends support to the claim by the mystic that he can achieve either a fully or at least a substantially unmediated experience -- one where the senses are all but shut down.

It is important to consider here the ramifications of a contentless experience. If in fact mystics across different cultures and religions are having contentless experiences that form the foundation of the overall mystical experience, then there is not only a striking similarity but even a sameness to the experiences that would seem to be beyond dispute. This has been elucidated by Norman Prigge and Gary Kessler:

> The negative definition of sameness, on the other hand, is completely applicable to unitive mystical experience. Two experiences, it will be recalled, are qualitatively the same if and only if they are not different, and they are different only if they have different qualities or aspects. But the only thing intrinsic to an experience that can have a quality or aspect is a content of consciousness. But since unitive mystical experiences cannot be or have a content of consciousness, there cannot obtain any difference between them, qua contents —and this, not because their contents are so similar, but because they have none whatsoever. And since two such experiences cannot be different, then, given the negative definition of sameness, they must be the same.

> The absence of difference between two unitive mystical experiences is absolute in two senses: first, it is a priori necessary rather than contingent for it is not that such experiences do not as a matter of fact have no differences, but that they cannot as a matter of definition; and second, it is in no way dependent on the purposes of the persons whose experiences are in question, for such purposes are germaine only to adjudging sameness and difference of contents and their qualities and aspects.[168]

Indeed, we can see that if the mystics' reports of a contentless consciousness are accurate, there is a sameness to the experience of mystics, no matter what their intent in seeking the mystical experience and no matter what their beliefs, concepts and personal makeup.

But, it may be argued, the mystics may be mistaken about their experiences, and the studies are neither conclusive nor do they support more than the content of the experience can be minimized. After all, when one is sleeping and yet later fails to remember his dreams, he has no ability to distinguish his dreamless sleep from the dreamful state, and likewise the mystic may think he is having a contentless experience, but it may have some amount of content. This scenario is certainly a possibility, but I think it does little damage to the overall claims of mystics. If in fact only minimal content and hence minimal mediation are present in the mystic experience, then we seem to have a strong similarity instead of a sameness. Moreover, the fact that so many mystics report the overriding and irresistible experience of unity lends support to that similarity, in addition to the similarity of the "power" of the experience.

Donald Rothberg has pointed out that mystical techniques are designed to deconstruct our ability to conceptualize and categorize, and that even if full deconstruction does not take place, at least significant deconstructed experiences seem to be achieved.

> They [meditative techniques and knowledge gained therefrom] seem, again following Forman and Brown, to involve a suspension of many modes of language and categorization, although this is not to say that all forms of mediation or conceptualization are transcended. Rather, such deconstruction occurs in what we might call a constructed or mediated manner. Still, the way of knowing does not primarily issue in linguistically mediated forms, that is, explanations and interpretations. Knowledge is here essentially a 'way of being,' a mode of experience in which categorization is drastically reduced and not active,. . . .[169]

Another option that we have already somewhat explored should be mentioned here. It seems possible that an experience with some content may be largely or even fully unmediated. This assertion is contrary to Katz's fundamental assumption that all experience is mediated.

For example, when a newborn baby first sees or experiences something new, is that contentful experience necessarily mediated? While it is mediated in the limited sense of being shaped by the baby's senses, it is largely or fully unmediated by the baby's prior experiences and beliefs because the baby essentially has none. It seems, moreover, that the newborn baby's prior experience and knowledge is not only minimal, but may be wholly irrelevant to the experience—so irrelevant as not to allow for any meaningful or significant mediation. The baby just does not have any relevant prior beliefs or concepts with which to influence or affect the new experience. In much the same way, the mystic who has minimized the content of his or her consciousness and who then experiences the undifferentiated unity—which is so different in kind from any prior experience that it precludes the relevancy and use of any prior concepts and beliefs in shaping that experience—would seem to have had an unmediated experience with arguably some content.

Likewise, the extrovertive experience of the nature mystic may be one that is full of the content of nature, and yet unmediated with respect to the unity experienced, since that unity is one that is so different from anything experienced before that all prior beliefs and concepts are irrelevant to the experience.

To sum up this point, it is at least plausible that one's consciousness could be "content-full" and yet a new experience can be so new and powerful as to be beyond any prior beliefs or conceptions of the subject. Such an experience would be an experience with content, but without mediation. If this is in fact what happens in some mystical experiences, then these experiences would seem to be "pure" and "raw" or "direct," and not mediated and therefore subject to scrutiny for subjectivity that unduly shapes or distorts the experience.

The concept of an awareness or consciousness that is unmediated and yet has content has been recognized in Indian Buddhist traditions and is called "Jnana." This has been translated as "unconstructed awareness," and has been contrasted with dreamless sleep, another type of unmediated consciousness, as follows:

> The difference between unconstructed awareness and such states [dreamless sleep] is that unconstructed awareness has both an object . . . and some content.[170] [emphasis added]

This idea of the possibility of a consciousness with content that has transcended any mediation or context of the subject is what Philip Almond seems to have in mind when he concludes his article on "Mysticism and Its Contexts" as follows:

> In the analysis of mystical discourse, we need to recognize that contexts may shape the nature of the experience by being incorporated into it. But also, because <u>mystical experience may transcend its apparent context</u>, we have to recognize that mystical experience may be decisive in the formulation of new, or the revision of existing, religious traditions, and this, <u>whether it be content-filled</u> or contentless.[171] [emphasis added]

Indeed, there is strong evidence that the mystics have a contentless and therefore unmediated experience, or, at a minimum, an experience of minimal content or mediation. Moreover, some experiences may be both contentful and unmediated. All this indicates that a similar experience among the mystics is quite possible.

C.   Challenge 3: Contentlessness vs. Unity.

A Katzian-like response to the claim that the mystic experience of contentlessness is unmediated and therefore the same or similar across cultures, is that the contentlessness is not the important aspect of the experience; rather, the unity and the ecstatic emotions or feelings of peacefulness or love, or the "seeing" of the Buddha or Christ are the significant aspects of the mystical experience. These experiences seem anything but contentless, and except for possibly the unity experience, are dissimilar experiences for the mystics of different religious and cultural traditions, too. Moreover, these experiences of the Buddha or Christ, or of ecstacy or peacefulness, are certainly mediated, and the experience of unity, being contentful, must also be.

In answering this charge, it is important to differentiate different stages of the mystical experience—an area where further research and comparison of mystical traditions is necessary. It seems to me, based on my review of many mystical reports, that the feeling of intense emotions and the mystic's "seeing" the Buddha or Christ, often come *after* the contentless experience. Certainly, as Katz has pointed out, there are elements of mediation present in these experiences. That is why it may be more likely that a Christian mystic will feel ecstasy while a Buddhist mystic will experience a sublime peace. All individuals have their own unique dispositions, fears, beliefs, ideas, reactions, and undertandings, and will respond to even the same initial experience in a different way. Katz is right to point out that the Christian mystic, the Sufi mystic, the Hindu mystic and the Buddhist mystic have different experiences, but those differences do not occur in the contentless phase of the mystical experience. As such, the fact that these latter stages of the mystical experience are mediated is not necessarily an impediment to the claim that one or more of the earlier stages are unmediated.

A much more difficult issue is whether the experience of undifferentiated unity is the same as the contentless experience, or is it also a later progression—a progression from the contentless experience to an experience with the content of unity? Put another way, is the contentless experience a "nonexperience," and if so, how could it be equated to an experience of unity? We might formally write the argument in premises as follows:

1.   For the "contentless experience" to be an experience, it must be different from not having any experience;

2.   If the contentless experience is different from not having any experience, then there must be some property that distinguishes it from the absence of any experience;

3.   The only way for an experience to have a property that distinguishes it from not having any experience is if it possesses some content;

4.   Therefore, the only type of contentless experience is a non-experience;

5.   The experience of undifferentiated unity has content and is therefore not a nonexperience;

6.   Therefore, the contentless "nonexperience" cannot be the same as or identical to the experience of unity.

While I will challenge the above argument, I believe the profound experience of unity normally occurs after the contentless experience, and if I am correct in this stance, then the above argument becomes irrelevant. With this in mind, some mystics can and do fairly equate the contentless and unity experiences as follows:

Premise 3 is open to a strong challenge, and Premise 5 is also challengeable. To understand what a contentless experience is, it would be helpful to read how it has been defined by contemporary philosophers. Robert Forman's book *The Problem of Pure Consciousness—Mysticism and Philosophy* consists of 12 articles that essentially argue that there is a common mystical experience across cultures and times. This commonality is called a Pure Consciousness Event (PCE).

Forman defines the PCE as "a wakeful though contentless (nonintentional) consciousness."[172] Paul Griffiths defines the PCE as "a mental event with no phenomenological attributes and no content . . . ."[173] Donald Rothberg states that "humans can at times be wakeful but in a way devoid of content and intentionality."[174] R.L. Franklin states that the PCE is a special case of the stilling of the mind that results in "a complete cessation of all thought, leaving a total quietness that is conscious and alert without being conscious of anything."[175]

The PCE is more thoroughly explained in the beginning of Stephen Bernhardt's article:

> The experience of pure consciousness can be characterized as follows: The subject is awake, conscious, but without an object or content of consciousness—no thoughts, emotions, sensations or awareness of any external phenomena. Nothing. During the event the subject is not even aware "Oh, I am experiencing X" or "I am having an extraordinary experience." Yet the subject is not asleep and may afterwards also report confidently that he or she was not asleep. Because one of the problems with the experience of pure consciousness is that it differs so radically from other types of experience, we may not want to call it an <u>experience</u>."[176] [emphasis added]

The reason we might not want to call the PCE an experience is that an experience is normally of something, while the PCE is an experience of nothingness.

Whether we call the PCE an experience or an event, my interpretation of the PCE is that it is an awareness or consciousness, even though at that time there are no objects of which it is aware. Franklin says that the mystic is "conscious and alert," Griffiths calls it a "mental event," and all agree that the subject is awake. A nonexperience, on the other hand, would not need or have consciousness, wakefulness, or alertness, nor is there any mental event at all. In this way, the PCE has the property of awareness or consciousness without having a content, and therefore is distinguishable from having no experience at all, thus defeating Premise 3 above.

An analogy may prove helpful here. Scientists tell us that in the universe there are vast areas of nothingness—areas where no atoms or molecules exist in space. Yet, this nothingness does have the attribute or property of being in various locations in space. If a spaceship crossed through this patch of nothingness in space, we would not say that the spaceship was nowhere, nor that the empty space in outer space had no existence. In much the same way, the awareness or consciousness on nothing or no object does not equate with no consciousness or nothingness; or, put another way, contentless awareness does not equal nothingness or a nonexperience. Similar to nothingness in outer space, which is experienced in time and space, the nothingness of the contentless experience is experienced in time. Indeed, the experience of nothingness is not the same as no experience.

Turning our attention to Premise 5, namely, that the experience of undifferentiated unity has content and therefore is not a nonexperience, we might well challenge that the experience of undifferentiated unity has content. If the undifferentiated unity is merely the way the mystic interprets or describes the alert awareness that has no object of consciousness, then we would conclude that it is contentless. Now the question arises as to why the mystic would later describe his or her contentless awareness as undifferentiated unity? In an experience not limited by categories or conceptualizations, with no differentiations to separate one thing from another, a description of an undifferentiated unity would seem to be quite descriptive indeed. Here we are seeing the ineffability of the experience influence its description, in that, in the attempt to describe the contentless experience or the experience without differentiation or categories, the mystic must use words that are finite and that use categories. The undifferentiated unity seems to be a plausible attempt to describe a contentless experience. Both the word "undifferentiated" and the word "unity" serve the purpose of conveying an experience that is free from distinctions and limited categories.

The above argument has shown that when some mystics use the term "the undifferentiated unity," they are probably describing the contentless experience, and further that there is no inconsistency in this since the contentless experience is an experience that is different from a nonexperience. Having said this, I believe that when most mystics use the term "undifferentiated unity," they are referring to a contentful experience that is distinct from the contentless experience, and usually occurs after and as a consequence of the contentless experience.

The reason for this conclusion is that the *profundity* of the mystical experience of undifferentiated unity does seem to indicate there is a content present. Put another way, an experience of nothingness alone would not be able to produce the reported and observed transformative effect on the subject—a transformation that has direction and often spurs the mystic on to engage in purposeful actions in the world. If the mystical experience were merely one of a contentless nothingness, on what basis or standard could any action that is undertaken be properly said to be based on this contentless as its source? Quite the contrary, the mystics who go beyond the contentless experience to the experience of unity are the ones who claim to have had a profound experience that has enough content to direct or shape their thoughts, attitudes and actions.

Indeed, it seems that many meditators may have had the contentless experience, but only a portion of them have had the profound experience of unity, and as previously stated, it is this profound experience of unity that is the essence or essential characteristic of the mystical experience, not the contentlessness, although the earlier stage of contentlessness is often the precursor of the experience of unity.

In fact, the introvertive mystical experience of undifferentiated unity does seem to usually result out of, from, and as a result of the contentless experience, although having the contentless experience does not guarantee a person of then experiencing this profound unity.

With this in mind, I would now like to propose a model of the progressive stages of many, if not most, introvertive mystical experiences—the deep experience that has changed the lives of those who have experienced it.

Stage 1:	The contentless experience or event;
Stage 2:	The unity experience;
Stage 3:	The feelings of profundity and emotion; and
Stage 4:	The specific religions or cultural aspect of the experience —such as "seeing" Christ or the Buddha.

What I believe most often occurs in the introvertive mystical experience is that from the contentless experience emerges the experience of unity, which is so powerful that it then affects the emotions of the individual, and thereafter in some triggers their pre-existing beliefs to produce an experience specific to them because it is based on their own religion, culture, language and background.

A few observations about this model of the mystical experience are in order. First of all, the contentless experience clearly seems to be unmediated since the self is transcended and there are no thoughts or perceptions to influence or be influenced.

The unity experience, although contentful, is at least arguably unmediated too. The contentless experience would seem to provide a "blank or clean slate," and it is at least plausible that an accurate, true and reliable experience is ripe for materializing. Put another way, when the mystic has transcended his context and gone beyond all mediation, as he does in the contentless experience, he may then be able to have a pure or raw experience of what exists—an experience that is likewise unmediated. This is in fact what the mystics claim, i.e., that the experience of unity is a direct experience of reality and is unmediated. The unity experience, therefore, would be the same or at least substantially similar cross-culturally since it is not mediated, or if mediated, that mediation would be only to a small degree. We should note here that Katz, while he might concede that if there is a contentless experience it is unmediated, would probably not concede that the contentful experience of unity is unmediated. We might, however, recall that since the unity experience is a limit experience, we should be mindful to be open to other and new explanations and standards for evaluating it, and take seriously the claim that the unity experience is a direct experience of reality that is unmediated.

When there is a recognition that the unity experience is profound, or when an emotional response to the unity experience occurs, the sense of self is no longer transcended, and at this point, mediation occurs. The mediation here is due to the type of person each mystic is—to the personality and/or psychological or emotional makeup of the mystic. The experience of the emotional Christian mystic may be one of ecstacy or love, while that of the stoic Buddhist or Hindu mystic might be of inner peace or quiet joy. These are reactional responses that are normally not directed by the mystic, but rather are what involuntarily occur as a result of the mixing of the unity experience with the mystic's own personality and makeup. The emotional response occurs as a human response to a meaningful, and sometimes shocking experience.

In the fourth and final stage of the mystical experience, there is a strong component of mediation, and the experience becomes more similar to those of mundane life in the sense that prior beliefs are utilized to shape and inform the experience. When Katz says that "the mystic brings to his experience a world of concepts, images, symbols and values which shape as well as colour the experience he eventually and actually has,"[177] he is certainly accurate in describing this final stage of the mystic experience where only the Christian sees Christ in his mystic experience, and only the Buddhist sees or experiences the Buddha. In this final stage, the Christian mystic does have a Christian experience, and the Buddhist mystic does have a Buddhist experience, but this is not the case in the earlier stages. A Christian and a Buddhist have the same contentless experience, arguably have the same or a substantially similar experience of unity, and may have a similar emotional response since the mediation in the third stage is more dependent on personality types and psychological or emotional makeup than on prior beliefs that are shaped by one's pre-existing religion and culture.

Indeed, Katz's focus on the fourth stage of the mystic process precludes him from seeing the sameness or similarity in experiences that seem necessarily to occur in the first (contentless), and possibly the second (unity) stages without regard to the background of the person or mystic having the experience. Katz's focus on the fourth stage also results in his glossing over the similarities and differences possible in the third stage that are a result of the emotional makeup of the subject more than his prior beliefs, concepts and language.

This proposed model of how the mystical experience works is consistent with mystical reports, and prior analyses of the stages of mysticism. For example, the mystic way is usually divided into three stages by Catholic theologians: The Way of Purgation, The Way of Illumination, and The Way of Union. The first stage of Purgation involves cleansing and purifying—what we might consider the loss of the consciousness of the self. The Way of Illumination deals with contemplation, and involves going beyond the senses and mental images. This should lead to the contentless experience. Thereafter, in the third stage, unity is experienced. My model has the additional stages that encompass when the experience of undifferentiated unity gives way to emotions or an experience of unity with God. It is in these latter stages where the mystic has passed into a mediated and interpretive realm that will produce differences between mystics of different cultures. Likewise, in line with my proposed model, in her book *Practical Mysticism*, Evelyn Underhill discusses stages of the mystical experience and clearly puts the emotional response of ecstasy after the contentless experience (which she describes as a place of darkness and quietude).[178]

Another point needs to be made regarding the stages of mystical experience. In the East, the contentless or unitive experience is usually considered the final stage, while in the West the contentless experience is an earlier stage that will subsequently culminate in union with God,[179] which I have stated is beyond the universal or common mystical experience, is mediated, and is therefore more open to challenge to any claims made regarding truth and reality. Some Eastern traditions, however, do seem to recognize that emotions often arise in the mystical experience, and instead of accepting those emotions as part of the final stage, attempt to dispense with those emotions to again enter a contentless experience. For example, Indian Buddhist meditation is classically described as having eight stages. The first stage involves the dissociation from sense-desires, the second stage involves dispensing with thought, and the later third and fourth stages involve the elimination of zest and then happiness.[180] It is after the initial contentless experience has been reached that all emotion is eradicated.

Several further points regarding the four stages of the introvertive mystical experience should be made clear. First, I am not suggesting that these four stages always occur, or that they always occur in this order, although I do believe that in the most advanced and profound mystical experiences, these stages do usually evolve as I have set forth.

Second, there is invariably an overlap between the stages. The second stage of unity is often present in and concurrent to the third stage of emotion and the fourth stage of religious/cultural content. This overlap may be one of the reasons that these stages of the mystical experience have not been previously delineated. Moreover, before Katz's bold assertion that all mystical experiences were mediated, the strong need and desire to make such distinctions did not exist. The unity experience does change as it is experienced in the later stages; it is undifferentiated in the second stage, but becomes differentiated in the third and fourth stages where concepts, categories and beliefs surface, and where the sense of self is no longer absent or lost.

Third, the fourth stage sometimes does not occur. It is possible to have an experience of the undifferentiated unity without the later infusion or development of religious or cultural content as a later stage of the mystical experience. Of course, when the mystic later reflects on his experience, the religious or cultural context and content do play an important role in the understanding and describing of the mystical experience.

It is also interesting to note that the Stage 1 contentless experience and the Stage 2 unity experience are both undifferentiated and beyond concepts, categories, and a sense of the self, but the first stage has no content and the second stage has a full content. More research and study are needed about how and why this transition from Stage 1 to Stage 2 takes place, and whether there is a difference in method, personality of the mystic, or some other factor that would account for the fact that only some people are able to progress from the contentless experience to the experience of unity.

In summary, although many mystics do have or inject content and emotion into their experience, this does not preclude a common contentless experience or a common unity experience that are the predecessors or precursors of the later emotions felt, and of the later mediated content. The mystics' reports of content in the mystical experience are neither inconsistent with the experiences of contentless and unity, nor do they preclude a striking similarity in the experiences of mystics, at least with respect to the first two stages of the mystical experience. Since the second stage of unity is normally considered the most important stage, there is a reasonable basis to conclude that mystical experiences are similar cross-culturally.

D.   Challenge 4: Dissimilarity.

In the prior section we have seen how differences in Stage 4 of the mystical experience do not preclude a similarity in the earlier stages of contentless and unity, and that a similarity in the unity experience across different cultures would in a very important respect make the overall experiences similar, since the experience of unity seems to be the central characteristic of the mystical experience and is what makes the experience profound and transformative. In this section we will explore a different model, one that is more general in that it will explain what it is that causes us to say one experience is similar to or different from another experience. We will again look at what Katz focuses on that leads him to find differences among mystical experiences. If, however, we focus on other aspects of the experiences, we may find similarities that either outweigh the differences or are more meaningful to us than are the differences.

We must first start out with the observation that no two experiences are alike. We may all see a blue fish, but the fish looks at least slightly different to each of us based on our own individual eyesight, the exact angle and distance we stand from the fish, and the different amounts of light that we see on the fish and that are striking our eyes. Although we may say we all see a blue fish, and we all do, we experience the image somewhat differently. The differences in this example are on the level of pure perception.

Let us proceed to an example where a seven-foot-tall Californian and a five-foot-tall Pygmy are both viewing a blue chair. Again, they would each see the chair differently because of their angles of viewing and their own visual abilities. If the Californian were color-blind, the chair would look significantly different to him than to the Pygmy.

Going beyond the level of mere perception, their experiences would be even more dissimilar if the Pygmy had never seen a chair before, and thought the chair was to be used as firewood, or as a step stool, or as a holder of objects, or as a toy to jump on or over. In each of these cases, the Pygmy would have a different experience than the Californian due in large part to a different interpretation of what he was viewing. The actual visual perception of the chair was only slightly different, the chair itself was no different for the two people, the emotional response to the chair may have been quite different, and the interpretation of the image of the chair was significantly different.

With this in mind, we can now answer what makes one experience similar to another experience. I propose that the four following criteria are what people usually consider when comparing experiences:

1.   Is the source, object or metaphysical reality of the experience the

same?

2.   Is a similar emotional reaction evoked?

3.   Is the mental image similar?

4.   Are the beliefs, attitudes and reactions towards the mental image similar?

If all four of these questions are answered "yes" by two individuals, then their experiences were quite similar. If one, two or three of the four questions were answered "yes," then there are similarities and differences, and the question then becomes which of the factors are more important in a given context. For example, if you and I both see different but equally heart-rending movies where we both cry, we might say we had a similar experience although the objects of the experience were different, and our mental images and beliefs about the mental images were different. If we are focusing on our emotional reactions, then the similar emotional response makes the experience similar for us.

If an ant and a person both look at a chair, their mental images have significant differences due to the differences between the sizes of the bodies and eyes of the perceivers; their beliefs, attitudes and reactions to the chair will be quite different due to the disparate sizes of their brains and each of their prior experiences regarding chairs; and the emotional responses are probably incomparable. The only primary similarity is that there is a chair that both the ant and the person are viewing, but this may be a significant similarity if the question of what was being experienced relates to what was present in the room.

If one person sees a mirage (sand that looks like water is present) and another sees water, the source of the experience, i.e., the objects seen, are different, but the mental image, beliefs, attitudes and reaction to the mental image, and the emotional reaction may all be the same. The two people had a similar experience in one sense, and yet a different experience if what is relevant is whether they experienced the same object or thing.

It should also be noted that there are significant gradations within criteria 2,

3 and 4. The mental images may be slightly different, somewhat different or very different, as is true for the beliefs, attitudes and reactions to the mental images, and the emotional responses.

As we may recall, Katz claimed that the Hindu has a Hindu mystical experience, that the Christian has a Christian mystical experience, and the Buddhist has a Buddhist mystical experience, and that the three experiences are necessarily dissimilar because of each of their pre-existing and differing beliefs and socio-religious-cultural and linguistic backgrounds. We have already discussed the mystic claim that the mystic's prior beliefs and background are transcended in the mystical experience, and if this is true, then the experiences of the Hindu and the Christian need not be significantly different, at least at the stages of experiences of contentless and of unity. The differences may only occur at a later stage where the self and prior beliefs are no longer fully transcended.

Additionally, Katz's constructivist challenge fails to notice the four criteria I have laid out for determining similarity, and likewise fails to account for the gradations possible within each criterion. Katz's contextualism primarily focuses on criterion 4, and to a lesser extent criterion 3, and seems to ignore criterion 1 -- arguably the most important criterion. Let us take an example:

Suppose that both a Christian mystic and a Buddhist mystic enter into meditation or contemplation, both experience a contentless experience, and then an overriding sense of unity, and *thereafter* the Christian "sees" an image of Christ and the Buddhist "sees" an image of the Buddha. Let us compare the experiences.

First, the later images were different, although the emotional responses may have been quite similar. However, the mystics in both traditions may well have earlier tapped into the same metaphysical reality of profound unity. In such a case, the experiences appear to be quite similar, although there are differences. Katz has chosen to focus on the precise image seen in the later stages of the experience as opposed to whether there is a similarity in the initial "object" or reality experienced, and to the exclusion of the emotional reaction. If the mystics are claiming to have tapped into a similar reality, how does Katz's stressing of the differences that may be due to the context of the mystic's religion or culture necessitate the conclusion that the experiences are predominantly different? After all, every experience is different from every other experience, but the more interesting question is whether the similarities are significant enough to properly conclude one is having essentially or in essence or to a significant and meaningful extent a similar experience.

Katz has emphasized that the Christian or Jewish mystic often interprets his experience as a merging or union with God, while the Buddhist mystic has no belief in God. Although this difference should not be glossed over, the overriding feeling of unity that is the essence of both experiences may be more important than the later differing interpretations of that experience or the later injection of prior beliefs. If both mystics are getting in touch with the same metaphysical reality, or even if both are initially experiencing the same contentless and then a similar feeling of unity, that similarity may be much more significant than the differing interpretations due to the different religious doctrines. Indeed, Norman Prigge and Gary Kessler have recently written,

> To be sure we often say nontrivially of two experiences (e.g., the aborigine's experience of a ballpoint pen and ours) that they are different because their contexts are different -- never merely because the contexts are different, but because they are different in a very significant way.[181] [emphasis added]

Moreover, it seems to me that in everyday usage when people are speaking of the similarity of experiences they tend to put the major emphasis on whether the object being experienced (the source of the experience) is the same, and yet Katz does exactly the opposite by usually placing the emphasis on the beliefs, attitudes and reactions of the mystics. This seems particularly counter-productive in the mystic context since the most important question is whether the mystics are tapping into a metaphysical reality or truth, not whether they color their experiences by their own contexts.

Although Katz's constructivism is a good explanation of why there were differences in mystical descriptions and to some extent in the experiences themselves, it is also true that a common source of the experiences would explain the similarities. This point was made by the foremost expert on Jewish mysticism, Gershom Scholem, when he wrote the following:

> Why does a Christian mystic always see Christian visions and not those of a Buddhist? Why does a Buddhist see the figures of his own partheon and not, for example, Jesus or the Madonna? Why does a Kabbalist on his way of enlightenment meet the prophet Elijah and not some figure from an alien world? The answer, of course, is that the expression of their experience is immediately transposed into symbols from their own world, <u>even if the objects of this experience are essentially the same</u> and not, as some students of mysticism, Catholics in particular, like to suppose, fundamentally different.[182] [emphasis added]

Katz would not agree that the experience is immediately transposed into the "symbols from their own world." Rather, Katz would assert that the experience itself is shaped and formed by the experiencer's prior beliefs, attitudes, disposition and his society, religion, and culture. However, the point I am focusing on here is that even if the mystic's concepts shape his experience, if the source or object of the experience is the same, then there is a similarity in the experiences in spite of the contextual differences, and that those similarities may be more relevant or important, depending on the focus and purpose of our inquiry.

This same point was clearly enunciated by F.C. Happold:

> Minds are conditioned by such factors as heredity, history, and environment, and further, are of varying quality. So the clear, but undifferentiated and formless vision, seen at the Primary level of awareness, as it passes through the medium of mind, is distorted and coloured. The result is, therefore, that we find different schools of thought, different theological and philosophical systems, different value-judgments, and different art forms. <u>What may be the same vision seen at the level of Primary awareness may be given a variety of forms as it is interpreted by differently conditioned minds.</u>[183] [emphasis added]

Again, Katz would seem to contest that there can be a primary awareness that is free from context, but the mystic claims that his experience of unity is just such a direct apprehension of reality and truth that is unmediated at the time.

In any event, Katz's constructivist analysis fails to account for the fact that all experiences have a context, and yet we consider many experiences to be similar to each other, especially if they are experiences of the same object, reality or truth. The context often plays a minimal role, while the object of the experience has the dominant position. When two educated Americans see a chair, their different contexts make little difference to the overall experience of the chair, and if one of the viewers were an educated Chinese Buddhist, the context would again play little role in the overall experience. The predominating factor or primary determinate of the experience would be the chair, not the context. I see no reason why the same should not hold true in the analysis of mystical experience. Now, I am not arguing that the mystical experience does tap into objective reality or truths, a subject that will be examined in Chapter IV, but if it does so, then that objective reality might well be more important and dominant in the experience than the mystic's context.

In that regard, the Katz claim that the mystical experience is mediated is a red herring. Mediation does not preclude a similarity in experiences. The great majority of experiences are mediated, and yet we certainly say that some of these experiences are similar to other experiences. Furthermore, when we find strikingly different contexts of the mystics and yet still see the presence of significant similarities in the experience, it is an indication that they may be tapping into the same metaphysical reality, albeit there are also other possible explanations for the similarity of experience (such as human makeup).

To make this point another way, Katz has placed undue emphasis on how beliefs shape experience, and has underemphasized how the object or reality experienced may be the most crucial aspect of both ordinary and mystical experiences. Moreover, the view that the object or reality or even perspective being experienced often has primacy over the context of the experience seems to best account for the common claim by mystics that the experience went far beyond anything ever experienced before, and was a difference in kind from all other experiences, not just in degree. It would seem that the mystic's context alone would normally preclude such a radically new experience, and a better explanation is that something is being experienced that is taking the mystic beyond his own context. This point is made by Robert Forman as follows:

> It should be clear that this is a fundamentally conservative hypothesis, that mystical experiences are created or shaped by long-held knowledge and beliefs, for example. But I do not think that such a conservative hypothesis can stand up to the data of mysticism. The history of mysticism is rife with cases in which expectations, models, previously acquired concepts, and so on, were deeply and radically disconfirmed.[184]

Mediation, quite probably taking place in all ordinary experience and at least in some mystical experience, should not lead one to the conclusion that there are no similarities in experiences. The pertinent question is whether the prior beliefs and concepts of the mystic lead him away from or toward truth and reality, or play little or no role.

In spite of the lengthy critique on Katz's constructivist thesis as he applies it to mysticism, Katz has made some good points. Katz has alerted us that differences in mystical experiences should not be glossed over, and that we must carefully evaluate which experiences are similar and which are not, or more precisely, which aspects of an experience are similar and which are not. Although the context of the experience need not be causal or determinative of the essential qualities of the experience, it certainly can and does play a role in many mystical experiences, and the philosopher should attempt to carefully see how significant that role was in each such experience. The more significant the differences present in the mystical experiences studied, arguably the more likely that metaphysical reality and truths are not being experienced.

Moreover, religious doctrines that differ between religions are hard pressed to claim validity on the basis of mystical experiences since those experiences are not uniform among mystics of different cultures. For that same reason, the notion of a personal God becomes suspect if it must rely on mystical experience for its support since the God-experience is not universal among mystics; many of the most accomplished mystics in the world come from a Buddhist background where a belief in God does not exist. This does not mean that the belief in a personal God or other religious doctrines are necessarily wrong, rather, it means that the dissimilarity of mystical experiences in these areas poses a formidable challenge to those who make such claims.

E.   **Challenge 5: No Self.**

Mystics often communicate both poetically and strongly when addressing the loss of the self as the self merges into the undifferentiated unity. Their statements, read out of context, seem to convey a loss that is contrary to common sense and fact. Indian mystics speak of the illusion of the self, as if we do not really exist. In Chapter 2, I quoted many mystics who seem to say that the self really goes out of existence. The following language has been previously cited: "You nullify your individual;" "Personal identity is lost;" "I passed away into nothingness, I vanished;" "The Perfect Man has no self;" "There is neither 'self' nor 'other';" and "I do not exist."[emphasis added]

These statements, however, are neither silly nor illogical when understood in their proper context. We should first acknowledge that most of the mystics whose communications have been recorded, and especially those who wrote their own words, were both educated and intelligent. They are attempting to convey an unusual experience, to put it mildly—one that is beyond the realm of ordinary consciousness and experience.

With this in mind, we cannot fairly attribute to the mystics that they believed their bodies disappeared in the mystical experience. After all, they are alive to tell us of the experience. Therefore, when they refer to the self they seem to be addressing something much deeper than the visible self we experience in everyday life, and that "self" we might call spirit, soul, or consciousness. Moreover, many mystics have acknowledged that although the sense of self disappears in large part, there is in fact a portion of the self that retains a trace of its individual consciousness so as to have the experience.

Meister Eckhart explained this loss of the self with a remaining trace of the individuality as follows:

> In this exalted state she has lost her proper self and is flowing full-flood into the unity of the divine nature. But what, you may ask, is the fate of this lost soul: does she find herself or not? My answer is, it seems to me that she does find herself and that at the point where every intelligence sees itself with itself. For though she sink all sinking in the oneness of divinity [*sic*] she never touches bottom. Wherefore God has <u>left her one little point</u> from which to get back to herself and find herself and know herself as creature.[185] [emphasis added]

Many mystics describe the loss of self as a loss of consciousness or self-consciousness, but not quite a complete loss. A medieval Christian mystic who did so was Henry Suso, who uses these words to explain the loss of self—a loss that is inchoate:

> When the spirit by the <u>loss of its self-consciousness</u> has in very truth established its abode in this glorious and dazzling obscurity, it is set free from every obstacle to union, and from its individual properties . . . when it passes away into God . . . . In this merging of itself in God <u>the spirit passes away and yet not wholly</u>.[186] [emphasis added]

Plotinus explains the loss of self in terms of freeing the mind of its finite *consciousness*, as illustrated below:

> You can only apprehend the Infinite . . . by entering into a state in which you are finite self no longer. This is . . . the liberation of your mind from finite <u>consciousness</u>. When you thus cease to be finite you become one with the Infinite.[187] [emphasis added]

Tennyson described his mystical experiences in terms of loss of consciousness, of individuality, and "loss of personality."

> A kind of waking trance -- this for lack of a better word—I have frequently had, quite up from boyhood, when I have been quite alone . . . . All at once, as it were out of the intensity of the <u>consciousness of individuality</u>, individuality itself seemed to dissolve and fade away into boundless being, and this was not a confused state but the clearest, the surest of the sure, utterly beyond words—where death

was an almost laughable impossibility—the loss of personality (if so it were) seeming no extinction but the only true life.[188] [emphasis added]

Recall my earlier quotation of Evelyn Underhill: "Your small self-conscious is lost in the consciousness of the Whole. . . ."[189]

Indeed, the "loss of self" is not a complete loss of the person, but rather is a temporary displacement of most of the individual consciousness into the consciousness of unity. There remains at least a small amount of consciousness or subconsciousness that enables one to be an experiencer of the unity experience. Just as a drop of water in the ocean is submerged and unified with the whole, but still "exists" in that it has not been destroyed or extinguished, so the loss of the sense of self or consciousness of self does not nullify the ability to experience.

The mystics do in fact understand the distinction between the feeling or appearance of the loss of the self as opposed to there really being a vanishing, disappearing or temporary annihilation of the self or person. Nelson Pike, in his study of Christian mystics, makes clear this dichotomy between the appearance and the reality regarding the loss of self, and concludes that the Christian mystics acknowledge only losing their sense of the self, not the actual self.

> Start with the idea that in union without distinction, the soul becomes "drunk" with love and thus loses track of the distinction between itself and God . . . . It is also what Ruysbroeck says in passages scattered throughout his writings—for example, in chapter III of *The Sparkling Stone*, where he claims that it is when the soul "is burnt up in love" that it "feels nothing but unity" with God. Still, although the inebriated soul can make no distinction between itself and God, distinction remains. What we need here is a distinction between appearance and reality. Identity is what *appears* to be the case; duality is what is the case in fact.[190]

> The soul then enters a state of "solitude" where it "loses itself," becomes "dead to itself," that is, loses track of the distinction between itself and God and thus is "as if, brought to nothing." This is the union without distinction where the sense of self has vanished.[191] [emphasis added]

82

Pike quotes a passage from John of the Cross in which John describes the mystical union of the soul with God, and following this quotation Pike explains the difference between how something appears to someone (phenomenologically), and what is the reality behind the appearance (metaphysically).

> The soul "appears to be God Himself." But the fact remains that the soul and God are not identical. *Phenomenologically* there is identity; *metaphysically* there is duality.[192]

This apparent paradox of the loss of the self with the ability to experience in spite of this loss has been well explained by Norman Prigge and Gary Kessler by making the distinction of "the self" as it is used in an "ordinary" or a "derivative" sense, i.e., whether the focus is on the self that is "extrinsic" to the experience and experiences it as such, or is "intrinsic" to the experience.

> An experience can have a subject also in either an ordinary or in a derivative sense. In the ordinary sense, the subject of an experience is the person having the experience. That person is part of the context of the experience and is extrinsic to the content of the experience. In the derivative sense, the subject of the experience is the awareness of self intrinsic to the experience. That awareness can be explicit or implicit. It is explicit in the case of self-conscious or reflected experience, where one is conscious of oneself having a content of consciousness. Thus, where there is no content of consciousness or (what has been seen above to be the same) where there is no object of the experience, there can be no explicit awareness of self. In the case of ordinary unreflected experience, where awareness of self consists solely in a sense of an otherness standing over against an object intended by the experience, therein the awareness is merely implicit or prerelective (as it is sometimes called). If, of course, there is no object of the experience—if, that is, the experience is not a content of consciousness—then there can be no implicit awareness of self standing over against an object. Consequently, a unitive mystical experience, neither being nor having a content of consciousness—having no object in any sense—cannot have a subject in the derivative sense. At the same time it must, of course, have a subject in the ordinary sense. Therewith the paradox of saying of a fully embodied mystic that his mystical experience has no subject is resolved. His mystical experience has a subject in the ordinary sense, a subject, however, which is extrinsic to the experience. At the same

time his experience has no subject in the derivative sense, no subject, or awareness of self, which is intrinsic to the experience.[193] [emphasis added]

F.   Challenge 6: Illusory World.

The mystics claim that they have experienced ultimate truth and reality—a reality and truth that is beyond anything we normally experience in our lives. Eastern mystics often refer to the ordinary, material world as illusory, unreal, or less real than the mystical realm. These claims have often made the entire mystical enterprise look questionable at best, ludicrous at worst. After all, how could any sane person deny the reality of our world? Moreover, to do so based on a rarely experienced and unseen world is to add insult to injury.

I think it is proper, here, to utilize the principle of charity and thereby assume (until given good reasons to think otherwise) that the mystic is intelligent and not making nonsensical claims. The mystic knows that there is a material world, and that people live in that world. The world is not illusory in the sense that it does not really exist. However, our consciousness about the world may in fact be quite "illusory" in the sense that it focuses on the superficial and not the primary, foundational or fundamental aspects of what exists. The mystic has experienced unity, and when the mystic experience is over he takes that profound experience into the world with him. Loving and helping others is an expression of unity. What the mystic sees, however, is a world focused on duality, multiplicity, hatred and selfishness. This world is not the world of unity, not an expression of the wholeness and oneness the mystic has experienced, and as such has been labeled less real or illusory. The mystic uses the word "illusory" in a different sense than it is normally used to illustrate an important point: Things are not as they appear to be. The world exhibits and displays multiplicity, but beneath it all is a more fundamental and foundational unity that is not apparent, much as the cells and atoms in our body are not apparent to our senses but are the very foundations of what is seen and experienced when we look in a mirror.

Happold expresses this point quite well in the following excerpt from his book titled, *Mysticism*.

> Man, however, lives in the illusion of multiplicity; he does not see the world and himself as they truly are; he is deceived by maya, a difficult term which is used with more than one meaning. In general, it is used to indicate the tendency to identify ourselves with our apparent selves and an apparent universe, to be deceived by the appearance which conceals the reality. It does not mean that the empirical world and the selves in it are mere illusions or are not, in their way, real; it means that they are not seen as, in their essential nature, they really are.[194]

If the mystics truly believed that this world was illusory or less real, they would have no inclination or reason to help others, and in fact would have no reason to lead a moral life since life in this world would be illusory. The contrary, however, is true; the mystics usually take their experience into the world to care for others. Buddhism has the Bodhisattva -- the mystic who has obtained enlightenment of the higher or ultimate truths and takes his experience and knowledge into the world where he performs virtuous acts of kindness, charity and compassion.[195] There would be no need to do this in a truly illusory world. Most mystics stress morals, and in that sense are not beyond good and evil as some have feared.[196]

The mystic is aware of the world of multiplicity, but brings what he considers to be the ultimate truth of unity into this world. He lives in both worlds, but believes one is made up of false appearance and the other of truth. On the other hand, the world of appearances is part of the whole. Underhill expresses the mystical awareness as follows:

> Now it is a paradox of human life, often observed even by the most concrete and unimaginative of philosophers, that man seems to be poised between two contradictory orders of Reality. Two planes of existence—or, perhaps, two ways of apprehending existence—lie within the possible span of consciousness. That great pair of opposites which metaphysicians call Being and Becoming, Eternity and Time, Unity and Multiplicity, and others mean, when they speak of the Spiritual or Natural Worlds, represents the two extreme forms under which the universe can be realised by him. The greatest men, those whose consciousness is extended to full span, can grasp, be aware of, both. They know themselves to live, both in the discrete,

manifested, ever changeful parts and appearances, and also in the Whole Fact.[197]

The mystic lives in the material world, but brings the world of unity and wholeness into the material world of multiplicity and appearances.

> [E]ach little event, each separate demand or invitation which comes to you is now seen in a truer proportion, because you bring to it your awareness of the Whole.[198]

The claim that the mystical experience of unity is more real or fundamental than everyday experiences is neither illogical nor clearly contrary to fact. Frits Staal has expounded on the fact that the mystic may be correct when he asserts that his characterization of reality as a unity may be more accurate than the normal characterizations involving multiplicity.

> A clear candidate for such a characteristic of mystical doctrines is the distinction between appearance and reality. All mystics assert that there is something real which lies beyond the appearances and which is not experienced under normal circumstances. They may then go beyond this rather general statement and present certain claims about this underlying reality—for example, that it is one, undifferentiated, or timeless. Such claims may become unintelligible, as we have seen. But there is nothing either in this general method and approach, or in such particular assertions, whether true or false, that is irrational or that conflicts with the law of noncontradiction. Of course, reality presents itself to us as plural, differentiated, and, at least partly, embedded in the flow of time. But this does not logically conflict with the possibility that deeper analysis might show that reality is in all these respects different. What would be illogical and irrational would be to claim that reality is at the same time one and many, or temporary and eternal; in Averroism, dialectics, phenomenology, or existentialism such claims are possible. [emphasis added]

> Not only is the distinction between appearances and reality consistent with logic and the requirements of rationality; it is in fact exactly what is presupposed in most sciences and all rational inquiry. Scientists have shown that objects which present themselves to us as solid are permeated by space; that things which appear near in space or time, empty, or young, are far, full, or old; and conversely, that

many events which appear in a certain way are quite different when subjected to deeper analysis. An illustration already referred to is provided by the distinction, in physics, between phenomenological and atomistic theories.

The distinction between reality and appearance, which science and mysticism share, is rejected by philosophies which confine themselves to "phenomena" as they present themselves, to ordinary experience, or to ordinary language.[199] [emphasis added]

Indeed, what is more or less real may be a matter of perspective, and from the predominating perspective of unity, the perspective of multiplicity in the world appears less significant and less real.

Chapter 4

Objectivity, Subjectivity, External Reality and Value

A.   Objectivity, Subjectivity and External Reality.

Considering the many philosophical papers written on mysticism, it is surprising how little the "objectivity" of the experience has been addressed. The mystics assume they have experienced reality and truth, and normally feel no need to present arguments to validate the experience they are so sure about. The constructivists and other skeptics of the mystical experience seem to get caught up in the question about whether there is a common core of characteristics that make up the mystical experience. Their belief in no common core puts any claim to metaphysical reality or truth in serious question for these skeptics. Moreover, the issue of objectivity is extremely difficult, and many may feel it is unanswerable, as are many philosophical and especially metaphysical questions. Having thus cushioned my foray into this difficult area, let us look into the "objectivity" of the mystical experience, and thereafter look at its relevance or value without regard to whether or not it can be deemed objective.

A Katzian-like approach to this issue might be as follows: Even granting that contentless experiences do occur across cultures, is that even important? A pure contentless experience alone gives us no insight into any truth or reality. Once the experience of unity begins, that experience is probably not of any ultimate or objective reality or truth, but rather, the best explanation is that the unity experience is the reaction of some people to a contentless experience. In that contentless experience where no limits or boundaries are present, an expansive feeling and experience of wholeness and unity is foreseeable, but this experience is due to human makeup and not any objective or metaphysical reality or truth. Even if one's prior beliefs are not forming or shaping the experience, a person's inherent makeup may be doing so. An individual's makeup causes him or her to dream, and even to experience dreams as real until awakened. What evidence is there for an objective reality that we cannot see, feel or touch, and that is not measurable or otherwise verifiable?

The mystic's response might be that the experience speaks for itself. Just as when one sees a chair or a car and "knows" they exist and are real, the unity experienced in the mystical experience is potentially verifiable by those who have the time and patience to cultivate their minds to stop their image-making and conception-making functions.

This response is probably unsatisfying to the skeptic, and for good reasons. Unity is arguably not something objective since it would not seem to have an ontological existence apart from the experiencer. One definition of "objective" in The Random House *Webster's College Dictionary* is "belonging to the object of thought rather than to the thinking subject." This appears to be what we are exploring here. It is similar to one definition of "objectivity," which is "external reality." But how can the mystic attribute "externality" to the unity experience? How can the mystic claim to be experiencing an "object of thought" when an undifferentiated unity might seem to preclude all subject-object discussion? One solution could be for the mystic to fall back on the Prigge-Kessler distinction of what is extrinsic or intrinsic to the experience, and conclude that the unity dissolves the subject-object distinction while in the experience, but from outside the experience there is a subject-object relationship.

This response then leads us to the next question: What is the object? Can an experience of unity be held to be an object? Unity is not an object like chairs or tables or people—it is not material. Unity cannot be measured for energy like the invisible atom, or even an emotion. So in what sense can we call the experience of unity an experience of objective reality or truth? Where is the "*object*" to make the experience *objective*?

At this point, I think it is important to recall the notion of a "limit experience." As discussed at the end of Chapter 1, there are experiences that are at the edge or limit of mundane or everyday experiences, such as the out-of-body experience or perhaps the still scientifically unexplainable experiences associated with E.S.P. (Extra-Sensory Perception), and it would be appropriate to consider judging those experiences with evolving or expanding standards. Even if this is true, the preliminary questions of whether the mystical experience is such a "limit" experience must be answered. In my opinion, a limit experience is one that is fundamentally different in a significant way from everyday experience, and because of that foundational or fundamental difference is not likely to be fully explained by the normal, accepted explanations. Such would seem to be the case for the mystical experiences of contentlessness and unity.

Ordinary experiences are all of something and have content, while the contentless experience is of nothing and contentless. It is fully or largely an unmediated experience where the sense of self is transcended. Although there is a subject having the experience, there is no object of the experience. As Katz and Kant before him have so artfully pointed out, everyday experience is of something, has content, and is mediated. The experience of nothingness is fundamentally different from the experience of something, and it is an unusual experience that normally requires great effort to achieve. Foundationally, the experiences of nothingness or of something are radically different. We would expect that when analyzing the objectivity or reality of the contentless experience, we would likely have to be open to new ideas and standards inasmuch as there is no object upon which the subject's awareness rests.

The profound unity experience, however, does seem to have a content, and if so, in this respect is similar to other experiences. That content, however, is unlike other content, which has categories, distinctions and differentiations. The undifferentiated unity, though contentful, is in some respects a state between contentless experience and normal contentful experience. Moreover, if the mystic's assertion is correct that the experience of undifferentiated unity is a direct experience of reality and unmediated, then it is fundamentally different from mundane experiences. If the transcendence of the sense of self continues in the stage of undifferentiated unity, i.e., if one's prior beliefs, conceptions, upbringing, etc., are still held in abeyance during the experience, then we have an experience that is fundamentally distinct from normal experiences, and an experience we would expect would have to be analyzed with altered standards.

A word of caution is in order here. Just because an experience is a limit experience does not mean we must throw away our rationality in analyzing and understanding it. We still should consider how our explanations of the experience fit in our overall belief systems. If our belief in the mystical experience would necessitate our giving up prior beliefs in our material world, then we would seem justified in rejecting such limit experiences, or at least explanations concerning their source and authority. A balancing act must occur in the application of every new standard or belief so that not only the new data are accounted for, but also prior beliefs that seem to be sound are not unduly discarded. While the limit experience should not be dismissed out of hand merely because it does not fit within our normal explanatory schemes, so too we should be careful not to accept standards upon which to judge the limit experience that would unnecessarily or improperly invalidate our other beliefs that appear well supported. It is within this framework that we should examine the mystical experience.

Turning again to the question of where is the *object* in the experience of unity that would allow the mystic to claim objectivity, we can readily see that there can be no material or physical object. If that is our standard, then the mystic's experience of unity will fall short of objectivity. However, when dealing in a realm beyond materiality, there may be realities and truths that cannot be measured against the same objective reference standard that we use with respect to things, but which nevertheless are not produced, generated, directed and controlled by us, and thus seem to have an independence and "otherness" to them that give them a type of objectivity if we utilize a more expanded definition of objectivity for this limit experience. The mystic's experience of unity may be real, although not of an object, nor verifiable by measurement.

What I am trying to convey here is that there may be an external reality that the subject is coming into contact with, yet because that reality is non-physical and non-measurable, it is quite unlike any other experience. It is neither subjective in the sense of being purely in the mind of the experiencer, nor objective in the sense of being of a physical object in the world or a presence that can be measured or quantified.

Let us now explore another way in which to view objectivity. All experiences, except possibly a contentless one, have a subjectivity component in that each one is experienced either by a different person or at a different time or place and hence, at least minimally different and personal than each other experience. However, there is strong evidence that both the contentless and unitive mystical experiences (if we wish to separate it into two) are the same or strikingly similar across cultures, traditions, religions and even eras. Is there not an "objectivity" to an experience when many people have a similar experience under similar circumstances?

One response to this line of argument might be that many people can be deceived or mistaken. For example, most scientists formerly believed that the world was flat; most people seeing a mirage in the desert for the first time and without the benefit of being told beforehand of such a possibility would have a convincing experience of seeing water; and most people interpret their dreams as real until they wake up, yet all are mistaken, at least temporarily, as to the reality of things.

I think, however, the mystical experience is somewhat unlike most other examples we could think of. Belief that the world was flat was based on a limited perspective, i.e., a view while on the earth, and in fact had its doubters due to the incongruity of certain physical laws with its conclusion of flatness. The mistake of perception regarding the mirage can easily be cured upon closer inspection. The

92

dream will at once be recognized as such by all sane people once they have awakened. The conviction of the truth of the mystical experience of unity, however, has not been shaken throughout the centuries, and no new view that seems to have any possibility of shaking that conviction has presented itself. Sane, intelligent people across many diverse traditions have had the conviction they have experienced ultimate reality and truth, and their experience has gone unchallenged by any counter-experience they have had, unlike in the above examples. Such mass delusion or illusion is certainly possible, but should not the nonexperiencer give the benefit of the doubt to the experiencer if that person's experience has been so uniformly "shared" by sane and intelligent persons?

Let us now change our approach on the issue of whether the mystic does in fact experience ultimate reality or truth—a truth that has some measure of objectivity. Let us look at several experiences to observe the differences between them regarding subjectivity-objectivity.

The first example is if we dreamt about a three-headed monster. The dream is an experience, but the experience is of something that does not exist. Because the object of the dream, or more generally put, the object of our thoughts, does not exist, we say that the dream is subjective and not objective; it is personal to us and was generated or created by us. There is no correspondence to any external reality.

The next two examples involve emotions. Here we must differentiate two different types of situations. If we were to see a movie that evoked an emotional response of sadness, we have elements of objectivity and subjectivity. The movie screen and movie are the sources of our experience; they are an objective, material reality that generated our experience of seeing the movie, which evoked the emotional response in us.

The sadness, however, would be based on our personal psychological and emotional makeup, albeit it may be true that this particular movie would evoke a similar response in many individuals. There is the externality of the movie and the internality of who we are that together create the experience.

The next situation involving emotions would be a thought or memory that evokes an emotion, such as the thought of the death of a loved one that produces sadness. Here, the thought is very personal to us, and was not generated directly by any material object. The thought exists and has an ontological status as a thought, but it is subjective in that it was generated by us. In this case, there was no movie screen or other material object that generated the picture or thought in our mind, and although the thought and the later emotion both may seem involuntary or a reaction over which we have little control, the fact is that we are the source of both the thoughts and the emotions experienced.

The fourth example to be considered is the contentless experience. This is the limit experience that is of no object and is unmediated. By having no object, we might well say it lacks objectivity, although it has a subject who is aware. However, the sameness of this experience among people of different cultures gives it a "scent" of objectivity in that it does not seem quite like a personal thought that is unique to the mystic. Although more could be said here, the next example is where the crux of the matter lies and to which we will now turn our attention.

The essential characteristic of the mystical experience is that of unity. Is the undifferentiated unity more like a thought that we generate ourselves, and as such, personal and subjective, or is it more similar to the experience of an external object, force or presence that we do not create or generate but rather "perceive" and, hence, that is more than purely subjective?

The mystics seem to assert that the unity they experience is so powerful that they have no ability to reliably generate it, nor do they feel in control of the experience during its occurrence, nor can they direct its shape or scope. Moreover, there is a clear feeling of "otherness" to it, in the sense that the mystic asserts no conscious direction or control. Indeed, the unity experience appears to be of a different kind and order than all other experiences, and the mystic has no knowledge or ability to reliably create, generate or manufacture such a novel experience.

Indeed, the mystical experience of unity has sometimes even come unsought and unanticipated, and the depth of the experience seems beyond any seemingly personal ability to generate it. As such, the experience itself has strong signs or markers of an external existence that is independent of the experiencer. Moreover, the experience does not appear to be based on the mystic's unique or subjective makeup. Furthermore, the overwhelming nature of the experience points to an outside source, and as such, may have an ontological reality and existence independent of the mystic. The fact that so many other people across different eras, cultures and religious traditions report what looks to be the same experience of unity over which no personal control or direction is perceived to take place lends further credence to the belief that there is an otherness to the unity that is independent of the subject-mystic. Indeed, it is somewhat similar to an objective experience in that the source of the experience is a thing that may generate a similar perception or experience in those who "perceive" it, although there is no object that can be perceived. The mystical experience may thus be more than subjective in that it may have an external source, and yet not be fully objective either.

Stace reached a similar conclusion to my own, namely, that the mystical experience may not be rightly labeled either subjective or objective -- though his analysis is certainly different from my own. He asked what it meant for an experience to be objective, and came up with two criteria: (1) an experience is objective when all normal people have the same or similar experience given the same conditions, and (2) the experience is orderly in all its internal and external relations.

We have already discussed the first criterion, but the second criterion and Stace's conclusions are worth considering. The second criterion is needed because people can be in agreement and still be in error. Two examples of the second criterion were given by Stace: dreams and crossing one's eyes.

Dreams sometimes are disorderly internally, as when people dream they can fly. This violates the natural laws. They may also dream they are in London, which is internally orderly, but if in fact the person is asleep in California, then the dream is externally disordered; it is contrary to the systematic order of the world.

When one crosses his eyes and thereby sees two images, he has achieved external disorder, since the same object cannot be in two places at once. Again, we see a law of nature or natural order violated.

Stace defines order as "the constant conjunction of repeatable items of experience."[200]

Stace contends that the contentless mystical experience cannot be objective because there is no way to find order since it is contentless; and likewise it cannot be considered subjective because there is no content with which it can conflict with natural laws and thereby be disorderly.[201] Stace concludes that the objective status of mystical experience with regard to reality and truth has "no solution of an intellectual kind and that it is part of the general mystical paradox that the mystical revelation transcends the intellect."[202]

Brian Fay has a very good discussion of objectivism and objectivity in his book *Contemporary Philosophy of Social Science*. He distinguishes between one's thoughts and what these thoughts are about, in the following words:

> The central point is the distinction between what is in our minds and what actually obtains outside of them. It is thus quite natural to think that in those cases in which the content of our minds is at variance with external realities this content is false; and that when the contents of our minds mirror what is outside of them these contents are true. Thus we come to think of knowledge as a kind of replication in which our mind's contents (how we represent reality) exactly reproduces reality as it is independent of us.[203]

It seems that the mystics would claim that the unity they experience is an independent reality, and thus not fully subjective. However, the question remains whether the mystic is correct in his evaluation of his own experience. Fay's further discussion may lend some support to the mystic in this regard:

> Knowing the difference between our mind and reality outside our mind, and wishing to make our mind accord with this reality in the sense of replicating it, how should we proceed? Isn't it obvious that the biggest impediment to matching our thoughts to reality are the distortions produced by our minds themselves? Our desires, our fears, our preconceptions -- these and countless other subjective

96

> elements -- befog our mind's mirror, clouding our mental vision and thereby preventing us from seeing reality lucidly. Thus we need to rid ourselves of these distorting elements as best we can in order to permit the light of reality to shine directly through to us. [emphasis added][204]

> These distorting elements are all subjective in the sense that they derive from us, the subject. If we could eliminate them these "subjective" elements would cease to have epistemic importance and the objects of our perceptions and thoughts would come plainly into view. Our statements and theories would then accord with the objects outside our minds, our beliefs would be "objective." [emphasis added][205]

Indeed, this is precisely what the mystics claim, namely, that they eliminate the distorting or subjective elements, that they eradicate their desires, fears and preconceptions, and thus are able to have an unmediated experience of external reality that is able to "permit the light of reality to shine directly through."

The mystic's method to learn the truth about external reality, that of eliminating the "self" and all of its subjectivity, is the ideal that Fay proposes for achieving objective truth.

> Since objective truth is achieved by ridding ourselves of deceptive mental elements, objectivity can also be defined as the cognitive state of lacking a priori categories and conceptions, desires, emotions, value-judgments, and the like which necessarily mislead and thereby prevent attaining objective truth.[206]

Fay's analysis indicates that the mystic's intentional endeavor to eliminate his sense of self is a step in the direction of objectivity, or at least a movement in the direction of experiencing an external reality. It does not, however, demonstrate that even if prior concepts, values and beliefs are eliminated that the "light of reality" will be experienced by the mystic, i.e., that the mystic is experiencing any external reality at all. This point is also supported by Fay's concluding remarks on this subject where he separates objectivity into two aspects, and it may be that only the second aspect of objectivity is satisfied by the mystic.

A theory or a fact is said to be objective if it fits with reality as it is in itself. Secondarily, persons or methods are said to be objective if they eliminate the subjective elements which typically prevent achieving objective truth.[207]

We have looked at evidence that seems to support the mystics' claims that they are eliminating the "subjective elements" by transcending their "self" in the contentless and possibly also the unitive stages of the mystical experience. But this is only a portion of the puzzle. The question remains as to whether the experience is more than subjective in that "it fits with reality as it is in itself."

Fay later questions the definitions of objectivity that I have heretofore set forth from his book, and offers this definition or explanation of objectivity:

> Objectivity does not consist of emptiness or disinteredness, as objectivism would have it; rather, it is the property of being detached from one's own commitments sufficiently to subject them to examination, of being sufficiently open to the possible merits of other viewpoints.
>
> *　　*　　*
>
> Objectivity conceived in this way is best termed *critical intersubjectivity*. It is intersubjective because it consists of an ongoing dialogue among rival inquirers each of whom attempts to understand the others in a manner genuinely open to the possibility that their views may have merits (indeed, more merits than one's own).[208]

This view of objectivity would seem to be especially helpful in the objectivity debate between skeptics, such as Katz, and the mystics. The skeptic should entertain the possibility that the mystic is having a limit experience that does tap into an underlying and fundamental reality of unity. Similarly, the mystic must also be willing to explore and examine other explanations of his mystical experience of unity—explanations that would not require the assumption of a reality or truth hidden from most of us. What this definition of objectivity requires is the best explanation for the source of the mystical experience of profound, undifferentiated unity.

Let us briefly explore several explanations of the mystical experience, first turning to alternative explanations to those given by the mystics, and then viewing one philosopher's argument as to why an underlying unity actually helps explain many things about the mundane world of multiplicity that we all experience.

The first explanation is referred to earlier in this section, namely, that the unity experience is the reaction of some people to the earlier contentless experience. An experience of contentless provides an escape and release from everyday worries, anxieties, fears, concerns, responsibilities and limitations that are present in contentful experiences. The contentless experience provides peacefulness like no other experience can, and moreover provides freedom from the limits, categories and boundaries inherent in all contentful experiences. This response or reaction of profound peacefulness and freedom is a foreseeable consequence of the contentless experience, and is consistent with the descriptions of undifferentiated unity. This experience of unity, although it may seem to have an otherness in that it is not consciously generated, is really just a foreseeable result or reaction based on human psychological, mental and emotional makeup, not an outside force or other outside reality. The mystics' explanation of the experience is an understandable mistake given the intensity of the experience coupled with its novelty and rarity. Emotions often seem to come upon us without our desire or control, but this no more gives them objective or ontological status than does the mystic experience of unity.

A second and similar explanation that could be given by the skeptic would be that the feeling of unity may be a feeling in all of us that the contentless experience allows to surface. We have the ability to dream of monsters and other objects that do not exist, to feel love or hatred for those we have not even met, and to experience unity given a certain set of conditions. We might say that unity is a latent part of ourselves that is rarely able to be fully experienced, but which sometimes flourishes as a result of the contentless experience. In this explanation, the experience of unity is not so much a psychological or emotional reaction to the contentless experience as it is the result of the "nourishment" of the contentless experience that allows the experience of unity to bloom. Again, a person's internal makeup and actions are the source of the experience, not an external other.

The skeptic can argue that these other explanations require no expansion of the prior standards, concepts and beliefs we hold, and are therefore the best explanation. The mystic can reply that while these other explanations are possible, they are outweighed by personal knowledge about the experience. The mystic can claim that he or she, having had the unity experience, is in a better position to judge its source. The mystic theoretically has the same ability of the skeptic to step back and judge the experience, and has the added perspective of the experience itself. To this, the skeptic can reply that although in theory the mystic's ability to neutrally judge the experience still exists, in reality the power of the mystical experience clouds the mystics' judgments and conclusions regarding the source of the experience, and that in any event these other explanations are more consistent with our other beliefs and are more convincing.

A philosopher who makes an interesting case for the presence of the external reality of mystical unity as the best explanation of the world in general, is J.N. Findlay.

> Mysticism, they think, is an attitude, deeply and widely human, which paints the world in peculiar, transcendental colours: these colours are an insubstantial pageant which reflects nothing deeply rooted in the nature of things.
>
> To counter this line of attack, I shall first argue that mystical unity at the limit or centre of things alone guarantees that coherence and continuity at the periphery which is involved in all our basic rational enterprises. Unmystical ways of viewing the world would see it as composed of a vast number of wholly independent entities and features, and this, as is well known, raises a whole host of notional quandaries, of ontological and epistemological problems. How can we form a valid conception of the structure of all space and time from the small specimens given to us? How can we extrapolate the character and behaviour of an individual from the small segment known to us? How can we generalize from the character and behaviour of one individual to the character and behaviour of a whole infinite class of individuals, wherever it may be distributed in the infinite reaches of space and time? Why, finally, do we think experienced things will have that affinity with our minds and our concepts that will enable us to plumb their secrets? It is well known that, on a metaphysic of radical independence and atomism, all these

questions admit of no satisfactory answer. Whereas, on a mystical basis, the profound fit and mutual accommodation of alienated, peripheral things is precisely what is to be expected: it is the alienated expression of a mystical unity which, however much strained to breaking point, never ceases to be real and effective.

Not only does Findlay think that an underlying unity is the best explanation for why human beings can understand the incredibly complex multiplicity in the world, but he goes on to say that this unity must be present for us to understand each other, and to even have similar views on morality and religion.

Much the same holds if we turn to that deep understanding of the interior life of others which arguably underlies all our interpretation and prediction of other people's behaviour, all acts of communication and co-operation, and all the ethical experiences and endeavours which arise in our relations with them. It is surely clear that unmystical views have the greatest difficulty in rendering these matter intelligible. They cannot make plain why we should be clear that others feel as we do in similar circumstances, and even how we attach meaning to such a presumption. They are forced to give unsatisfactory, behaviouristic analyses of what we are so sure of, or justify our certainty in strange left-handed ways. Whereas, on a mystical basis, our understanding of others rests on the fact that they are not absolutely others, but only variously alienated forms of the same ultimate, pervasive unity, which expresses itself in the inkling, whether clear or remote, of what may be present in the experience of others. And alienation, however profound, is something that could be surmounted at a sufficiently high degree of mystical *approfondissement*, at which levels the puzzles of the *Blue Book* or the *Philosophical Investigations* would be not so much solved as dissolved. All our higher valuations of impersonal benevolence, of justice, of knowledge, of beauty, of virtue are, further, attitudes having their roots in a transcendence of the separate individual and his contingent interests, and in a rise to higher-order interests which make an appeal to everyone and consider the state of everyone. The supreme dignity and authority of these valuations is much more understandable on a mystical than on an unmystical basis: a moralist like Schopenhauer, for example, bases all morality on a profound suprapersonal identity. The attempts of unmystical people like Hare or even Ross to write books on the foundations of ethics is not anything that encourages imitation. I should say, lastly, that the deep meaning and also the absurdities of various religious systems are best

> understood on a mystical basis, and totally unintelligible on an unmystical basis. This applies particularly to our own family of Semitic religions. What readily appears as an unedifying series of myths about the arbitrary acts of an external being, involving much ritual effusion of blood and legalistic substitution, becomes understandable when seen as expressing the profound unity, despite alienation, of the finite human person with the principle of all being and all excellence.[209]

I will leave it to the reader to decide how persuaded they are by Findlay's "best explanation" for the mystical experience.

I believe we have now laid a foundation for a method that addresses the issue of the source of the mystic experience. We should first agree that there is substantial evidence that the mystic is able to largely or even fully transcend his prior concepts, desires, beliefs and cultural-religious background. I think we should also agree that the mystical experience is a limit experience that may not fall within a definition of objectivity that requires an external "object" that is experienced, but that may be tapping into an "otherness" that would make it more than a purely subjective experience. The issue then remains as to what is the best explanation of the mystical experience of unity. Is it human predisposition, is it a consequence of the contentless experience that is related to our internal makeup, is it a tapping into the "otherness" of undifferentiated unity, or is there some other explanation? Katz and many others have seemed to preclude such an inquiry by presupposing that the mystic does not have an unmediated experience. However, even mediated experiences can have an outside object as its source, and the mystical experience may well be either unmediated or be mediated to only a limited degree. It is time for investigators to shed their initial overriding skepticism about something they have not experienced and which thereby precludes them from fairly entertaining and examining the mystics' interpretation of their own experience, and then to compare that explanation with other reasonable explanations.

While the mystics' claims should not be summarily dismissed, neither should they be blindly accepted. This book is a call for philosophers to look with an open mind at the possible explanations for the source of the mystical experience, and to ponder what is the best explanation of the source of those experiences. Too much of the prior literature that analyzes the mystical experience has been unduly tainted with a bias or prejudice for or against the mystics' interpretation of the source of the experience. Neither side of the debate seems to have displayed the "objectivity" or "neutrality" that it has accused the other side of ignoring. It is indeed ironic that in attempting to determine whether the mystical experience is of an external reality or "objective," the analysts themselves have often failed to be objective. The result has more often been self-serving conclusions instead of hard, philosophical analysis. It is time to remedy this.

B.   Value.

Whether or not the mystic gets in touch with or experiences an external reality, I believe that the mystical experience has tremendous value for the mystic and for society. The following comment from Stace helps bring home the distinction between truth or objectivity on one hand, and value on the other hand.

> The philosopher who holds the opinion that moral and aesthetic values are subjective—as being grounded in emotions or attitudes—does not mean to say that these values are not valuable, or that morality and art ought to be left behind as superstitious! It ought to be obvious that the same is true of the values of mystical experience.[210]

Mysticism has value in at least three distinct ways: (1) on an emotional level; (2) in providing new perspectives; and (3) in providing better, superior or more important perspectives.

First, as to the emotional value of mystical experience, we may recall the joy, ecstasy and/or peace that so many mystics experience, and the intensity and depth of those emotions. Moreover, incredible expansion, freedom and elation are the consequences of the contentless experience that has no limits or borders. Furthermore, the deep sense of profundity and the experience of reality and truth provide the mystic great comfort and security in an insecure world. These are all substantial and invaluable benefits to the individuals having the mystical experience, and should neither be disparaged nor discounted easily.

The emotional benefits, however, cannot be viewed in a vacuum. The mystical life is difficult and challenging, involving countless hours of meditation or selfless service without any guarantee of having the mystical experience. As mentioned earlier, sometimes the experience of the void or nothingness produces great fear, since the experience is of the unseen and unknown. The tremendous benefits seem to greatly outweigh the costs, but efforts and obstacles must be made and faced; as is true in many aspects of life, what is worthwhile rarely comes effortlessly or painlessly.

Second, the mystical unitive experience provides the individual with new perspectives and provides the mystic with new ways to behave, act and be in the everyday world. The person often is no longer reactive to and upset by the common trials and tribulations within which most people become so enmeshed and embroiled, having tasted a unity and wholeness that provide a bigger picture than the often petty, selfish and self-centered concerns on which most of us waste so much energy. He is able to be patient and loving, where before, he may have been impatient and insensitive to the plight of others. These new perspectives are of personal benefit in that he can channel his energies in a productive manner and live a more fulfilling and enriched life. His friends and his society will inevitably benefit from his ability to take his unity experience and bring it into the world of multiplicity. His unity experience has added a great deal and allowed him to be a more complete individual. That completeness, moreover, opens up new possibilities for him, and provides new avenues for the mystic to live a creative and meaningful life. These new perspectives are in addition to the old perspectives, and thus the mystic has gained and added to what he already had and still has. His life is now expanded, and that expansion touches the people with whom he comes into contact.

Evelyn Underhill has quite beautifully described this addition and enrichment that the mystical experience provides.

>Their [the mystics'] attention to life has changed its character, sharpened its focus: and as a result they see, some a wider landscape, some a more brilliant, more significant, more detailed world than that which is apparent to the less educated, less observant vision of common sense.[211]

>Each new stage achieved in the mystical development of the spirit has meant, not the leaving behind of the previous stages, but an adding on to them; an ever greater extension of experience, and enrichment of personality. So that the total result of this change, this steady growth of your transcendental self, is not an impoverishment of the sense-self in the supposed interests of the super-sensual, but the addition to it of another life—a huge widening and deepening of the field over which your attention can play.[212]

>You will hardly deny that this is a practical gain: that this widening and deepening of the range over which your powers work makes you more of a man than you were before, and thus adds to rather than subtracts from your total practical efficiency. It is indeed only when he reaches these levels, and feels himself within this creative freedom—this full actualisation of himself—that man becomes fully human. . . .[213]

Third, mysticism provides not only new insights and perspectives, but in many ways better, superior and/or more important perspectives than those of the nonmystic. I realize this is a bold statement, for if there is no "objectivity" to the mystical experience, how can it be deemed that mystical perspectives are important, or superior to other perspectives? I think, however, that in much the same manner as one action is judged better, or one painting is judged superior to another, that the perspectives learned in, through and from the mystical experience can be viewed as superior and vitally important. Let me give a few illustrative examples.

If sight were given to a blind man, in many respects he would feel he had gained something of importance and superiority to what he has had. The adding of something new, useful, and pleasing—something that can help him more deeply and thoroughly connect with his fellow man and the world—this addition can be seen as an improvement and as superior. We usually consider something to be superior or better if it allows us to do more things or lead a more complete, full, and enriched life. Both the gaining of sight and the gain resulting from the unitive experience can be seen in this way.

Another more controversial example may be instructive. When we dream, we have an experience—a dream experience. We call this experience less real than the experience of waking consciousness. In waking consciousness we can do things that we only dream about in our dreams. The mystic takes his sense of unity and is able to accomplish things in the world that arguably cannot be accomplished from other perspectives. An example might be Gandhi's nonviolent "actions" that led to the independence of India and the freedom of hundreds of millions of people. Whether or not Gandhi was a mystic, he did live his life from the mystical perspective of unity—of respect for even the oppressor, of love over hatred, and of nonviolence over violence—and his perspectives and actions led to a freedom that was accomplished with minimal loss of life and a sense of dignity and goodwill that would not otherwise have been possible. After all, we in the Western world look at the peaceful transition of power from one administration to the next as superior to the violent coups that take place throughout much of the undemocratic world. That peaceful way of deciding things is in accord with the mystical experience of unity, and in some ways seems more real and important to our lives than the common way of resolving disputes by power and force. Much as a dream is perceived as less real and less important and inferior to waking consciousness, so a consciousness of unity can be considered to be superior to a consciousness of divisiveness, hate, duality and multiplicity.

One could argue that all true human advancement, as opposed to technological advancement, has been as a result of living a life of unity. For example, at one time not so very long ago, men ate other men. Unity demands the respect for other human beings, and cannibalism is in fact a great example of selfishness and self-centeredness at the expense of others. Unity would never allow for such actions.

Indeed, unity could be said to be a superior perspective for several reasons:

(1) this would be a better world if all people lived a life based on unity; (2) this has been and is a better world because some people live a life based on unity; and (3) this has been and is a better world because some of our greatest people and role models have lived their lives based on unity.

The first point is theoretical, but I believe it is quite evident that if all people lived a life where love, caring and concern for others were priorities, this world would not only be better from a practical standpoint, but people would live more enriched and fulfilled lives. Humans are social animals, and to help and be helped by others, to live and be loved by others, to care and be cared for by others, to think of and be thought of by others—this is the type of life that generates happiness, satisfaction, fulfillment and inner peace. Of course, if all people lived their lives based on unity, hunger and poverty would in fact be greatly diminished or eliminated.

Second, who among us has not benefited from the kindness and assistance of others? The Boddhisattva, the Buddhist mystic who has experienced unity, lives his life solely to benefit others. Who is not the better for having experienced the Boddhisattva's help? We are grateful when we are fortunate enough to come into contact with a person who sees the goodness in us and in everyone, and who helps and loves each person unconditionally.

Last, this world seems a better place because of the lives of great people who have lived their lives based on unity: Jesus Christ, the Buddha, Gandhi, Martin Luther King Jr., Mother Teresa, to name a few. These people serve as inspirations and models for what a life based on unity looks like and can be.

It might be pointed out that many people have lived lives based on unity without having had a mystical experience. This claim is undoubtedly true, but the mystic who has experienced the overpowering unity where there is no multiplicity seems best able to grasp and live such a life. Most of us live our lives based on what we "feel" deep down, not on intellectual grounds alone. All people know that to be overweight or to smoke is not good for their health, but few can permanently alter their behavior based on only intellectual realization. The mystical experience—with its depth and breadth—literally transforms the subject so that he lives a different life and is a different person. The experience of undifferentiated unity is then able to be carried into the material world and lived as a differentiated unity.

On the other hand, it is also true that having a mystical experience in no way ensures that one will live a mystical life based on unity. The world of duality and multiplicity, with temptation and desire, are realities that the mystic, as a human being, must face. The mystical experience is so powerful, however, that worldly challenges are often able to be met from the mystical perspective of unity.

The enormous value of the mystical experience and the mystical way of life was recognized by Bertrand Russell, who, although skeptical about mystical claims of experiencing ultimate truth, was nonetheless convinced of their ability to inspire man in a unique and unsurpassed way.

> [T]here is an element of wisdom to be learned from the mystical way of feeling, which does not seem to be attainable in any other manner. If this is the truth, mysticism is to be commended as an attitude towards life, not as a creed about the world. The metaphysical creed, I shall maintain, is a mistaken outcome of the emotion, although this emotion, as colouring and informing all other thoughts and feelings, is the inspirer of whatever is best in man."[214] [emphasis added]

Indeed, the mystical experience of unity has substantial value not only to the individual mystic, but also for his friends and his society as a whole. It is an enriching experience that involves an expansion into new perspectives, and in that respect opens up whole new worlds. Whether or not there is such a thing as ultimate truth, a life lived from unity would seem to provide ultimate value to the one and the all, and unless and until we have had the mystical experience of unity ourselves, we should not be too hasty to condemn the mystics' claims of experiencing enlightening and fundamental levels and aspects of truth and reality.

References

1. F.C. Happold, *Mysticism*, Penguin Books, 1963, p.121.

2. S.N. Dasgupta, *Hindu Mysticism*, Motilal Banarsidass, 1927, preface p. IX.

3. Bertrand Russell, *Mysticism and Logic*, Penguin Books, 1918, p. 9.

4. W.T. Stace, *Mysticism and Philosophy*, London: Macmillan Press, 1960, pp.162-163.

5. R.L. Franklin, "Experience and Interpretation in Mysticism" in *The Problem of Pure Consciousness*, edited by Robert Forman, Oxford University Press, 1990, pp. 296-297.

6. Donald Rothberg, "Contemporary Epistemology and the Study of Mysticism" in *The Problem of Pure Consciousness, supra*, n. 5, p. 165.

7. W.T. Stace, *supra*, n. 4, pp. 204-205.

8. W.T. Stace, *supra*, n. 4, pp. 33-34.

9. Peter Moore, "Mystical Experience, Mystical Doctrine, Mystical Technique" in *Mysticism and Philosophical Analysis*, edited by Steven T. Katz, Oxford University Press, 1978, p. 101.

10. Donald Rothberg, *supra*, n. 6, pp. 164-165.

11. R.L. Franklin, *supra*, n. 5, p. 290.

12. Robert K.C. Forman, "Introduction: Mysticism, Constructivism, and Forgetting" in *The Problem of Pure Consciousness, supra*, n. 5, p. 3.

13. Donald Rothberg, *supra*, n. 6, pp. 171-172.

14. Steven Katz, "Language, Epistemology and Mysticism" in *Mysticism and Philosophical Analysis, supra*, n. 9, pp. 22-66.

15. *Ibid*, pp. 26-27.

16. *Ibid*, p. 27.

17. *Ibid*, p. 30.

18. *Ibid*, p. 46.

19. *Ibid*, p. 40.

20. *Ibid*, p. 33.

21. *Ibid*, p. 22

22. Philip Almond, in his article "Mysticism and Its Contexts," similarly lays out Katz's methodological stance as follows: (1) There are no unmediated experiences; and therefore (2) The context of mystical experience is determined by the religious tradition in which it occurs; consequently, (3) There are as many different types of mystical experience as there are religious traditions in which they occur. *The Problem of Pure Consciousness, supra*, n. 5, p. 211.

23. Stephen Bernhardt, "Are Pure Consciousness Events Unmediated?" in *The Problem of Pure Consciousness, supra*, n. 5, p. 227.

24. J.N. Findlay, *Ascent to the Absolute*, Humanities Press, 1970, p.174.

25. Evelyn Underhill, *Practical Mysticism*, Ariel Press, 1914, p. 23.

26. Gershom Scholem, *On the Kabbalah and Its Symbolism*, Schocken Books, 1965, p. 5.

27. R.L. Franklin, *supra*, n. 5, p. 289.

28. S.N. Dasgupta, *supra*, n. 2, p. 17.

29. R.C. Zaehner, *Sacred and Profane*, Clarendon Press, 1957, Oxford University Press, 1961, p.198.

30. W.T. Stace, *supra*, n. 4, pp.131-132.

31. Robert M. Gimello, "Mysticism and Meditation" in *Mysticism and Philosophical Analysis, supra*, n. 9, p.178.

32. Carl A. Keller, "Mystical Literature" in *Mysticism and Philosophical Analysis, supra*, n.9, p.95.

33. Peter Moore, *supra*, n. 9, p.119.

34. R.C. Zaehner, *supra*, n. 29, pp.172-173.

35. S.N. Dasgupta, *supra*, n. 2, p. 55.

36. Evelyn Underhill, *supra*, n. 25, p. 40.

37. W.T. Stace, *supra*, n. 4, p. 50.

38. *Ibid*, p. 88.

39. Lao-Tzu, *Tao Te Ching*, Alfred A. Knopf, Everyman's Library, 1994, translation by D.C. Lau, edited by Sarah Allan, T. Ching 19.

40. F.C. Happold, *supra*, n.1, p. 212.

41. *Ibid*, p. 223.

42. *Ibid*, p. 379.

43. Evelyn Underhill, *supra*, n. 25, p.138.

44. *Ibid*, p. 28.

45. S.N. Dasgupta, *supra*, n. 2, pp. 40-41.

46. *Ibid*, p. 70.

47. F.C. Happold, *supra*, n.1, p.163.

48. *Ibid*, p. 212.

49. *Ibid*, p. 361.

50. Lao-Tzu, *supra*, n. 39, Te Ching 10.

51. *Ibid*, Te Ching 28.

52. *Ibid*, Te Ching 31.

53. *Ibid*, Tao Ching 64.

54. Chuang Tzu, *Chuang Tzu Basic Writings*, Columbia University Press, 1964, translated by Burton Watson, p. 54.

55. W.T. Stace, *supra*, n. 4, p. 57.

56. Evelyn Underhill, *supra*, n. 25, pp.167-168.

112

57. Daniel Matt, *The Essential Kabbalah*, Castle Books, 1995, p.124.

58. W.T. Stace, *supra*, n. 4, p.115.

59. F.C. Happold, *supra*, n.1, p. 251.

60. *Ibid*, p. 258.

61. Chuang Tzu, *supra*, n. 54, p. 26.

62. Christopher Chapple, "The Unseen Seer and The Field: Consciousness in Samkhya and Yoga" in *The Problem of Pure Consciousness, supra*, n.5, p.59.

63. F.C. Happold, *supra*, n.1, p.168.

64. *Ibid*, p. 275.

65. W.T. Stace, *supra*, n. 4, pp. 61-62.

66. *Ibid*, p. 64.

67. *Ibid*, p. 49.

68. *Ibid*, p.132.

69. *Ibid*, p. 49.

70. *Ibid*, p. 60.

71. *Ibid*, p. 86.

72. *Ibid*, p.110.

73. William James, "Mysticism" in *The Varieties of Religious Experience*, 1902, p. 379.

74. *Ibid*, p. 407.

75. *Ibid*, p. 410.

76. S.N. Dasgupta, *supra*, n. 2, pp. 41-42.

77. W.T. Stace, *supra*, n. 4, p. 94.

78. *Ibid*, p. 97.

79. Daniel Matt, *supra*, n. 57, p. 29.

80.   *Ibid*, p. 63.

81.   *Ibid*, p. 69.

82.   William James, *supra*, n. 73, p. 411.

83.   Chuang Tzu, *supra*, n. 54, p. 35.

84.   *Ibid*, p. 36.

85.   *Ibid*, p. 38.

86.   Nelson Foster and Jack Shoemaker, *The Roaring Stream*, The Ecco Press, 1996, p. 38.

87.   *Ibid*, p. 91.

88.   *Ibid*, p. 214.

89.   *Ibid*, pp. 226-227.

90.   Lao Tzu, *supra*, n. 39, Tao Ching 48.

91.   *Ibid*, Tao Ching 60.

92.   Foster and Shoemaker, *supra*, n. 86, p. 38.

93.   *Ibid*, p. 46.

94.   Chuang Tzu, *supra*, n. 54, p. 39.

95.   W.T. Stace, *supra*, n. 4, p. 66.

96.   William James, *supra*, n. 73, p. 371.

97.   *Ibid*, p. 371.

98.   Evelyn Underhill, *supra*, n. 25, p.162.

99.   Frederick Streng, "Language and Mystical Awareness" in *Mysticism and Philosophical Analysis, supra*, n. 9, p.142.

100. R.C. Zaehner, *supra*, n. 29, p. 50.

101. F.C. Happold, *supra*, n.1, p. 354.

102. Lao Tzu, *supra*, n. 39, Te Ching 27.

114

103. *Ibid*, Tao Ching 63.

104. Chuang Tzu, *supra*, n. 54, p. 52.

105. *Ibid*, p. 36.

106. *Ibid*, p. 77.

107. *Ibid*, p. 58.

108. *Ibid*, p.104.

109. *Ibid*, p. 41.

110. William James, *supra*, n. 73, p. 406.

111. F.C. Happold, *supra*, n.1, p. 361.

112. Frederick Streng, *supra*, n. 99, p.143.

113. R.C. Zaehner, *supra*, n. 29, Introduction p. XIII.

114. F.C. Happold, *supra*, n.1, pp. 352-353.

115. S.N. Dasgupta, *supra*, n. 2, p. 39.

116. Robert Gimello, *supra*, n. 31, p.178.

117. F.C. Happold, *supra*, n.1, p. 39.

118. *Ibid*, pp. 265, 267.

119. R.C. Zaehner, *supra*, n. 29, p.155.

120. Evelyn Underhill, *supra*, n. 25, pp.156-157.

121. *Ibid*, p.148.

122. *Ibid*. p.175.

123. William James, *supra*, n. 73, p. 371.

124. Lao-Tzu, *supra*, n. 39, Tao Ching 45.

125. *Ibid*, Tao Ching 76, 81.

126. *Ibid*, Te Ching 19.

127. Foster and Shoemaker, *supra*, n. 86, p. 61.

128. *Ibid*, p. 91.

129. *Ibid*, p.112.

130. F.C. Happold, *supra*, n.1, p. 217.

131. *Ibid*, p. 275.

132. William James, *supra*, n. 73, p. 372.

133. *Ibid*, p. 372.

134. W.T. Stace, *supra*, n. 4, p.110.

135. R.C. Zaehner, *supra*, n. 29, p. 41.

136. W.T. Stace, *supra*, n. 4, p. 99.

137. Robert Gimello, *supra*, n. 31, p.178.

138. Frits Staal, "The Alleged Irrationality of Mysticism" in *Exploring Mysticism*, 1975, p. 27.

139. *Ibid*, pp. 28-29.

140. Frederick Streng, *supra*, n. 99, p.166.

141. Frits Staal, *supra*, n.138, p. 31.

142. *Ibid*, p. 30.

143. *Ibid*, p. 58.

144. Peter Moore, *supra*, n. 9, p.102.

145. Steven Katz, *supra*, n.14, p. 54.

146. F.C. Happold, *supra*, n.1, p. 339.

147. Daniel Matt, *supra*, n. 57, p. 29.

148. Frederick Streng, *supra*, n. 99, p.159.

149. Gershom Scholem, *supra*, n. 26, p. 8.

116

150. W.T. Stace, *supra*, n. 4, pp. 285-288.

151. Robert K.C. Forman, *supra*, n.12, p. 41.

152. Frits Staal, *supra*, n.138, pp. 45-46.

153. Norman Prigge and Gary Kessler, "Is Mystical Experience Everywhere the Same?" in *The Problem of Pure Consciousness, supra*, n. 5, pp. 278-279.

154. W.T. Stace, *supra*, n. 4, pp. 297-298.

155. Steven Katz, *supra*, n. 14, pp. 25-26.

156. Paul J. Griffiths, "Pure Consciousness and Indian Buddhism" in *The Problem of Pure Consciousness, supra*, n. 5, p. 78.

157. S.N. Dasgupta, *supra*, n.2, p. 62, and Christopher Chapple, *supra*, n.64, p. 63.

158. S.N. Dasgupta, *supra*, n. 2, p. 88.

159. Robert K.C. Forman, "Eckhart, Gezucken and the Ground of the Soul" in *The Problem of Pure Consciousness, supra*, n. 5, p.106.

160. W.T. Stace, *supra*, n. 4, p.109.

161. Donald Rothberg, *supra*, n. 6, p.183.

162. Robert K.C. Forman, *supra*, n.12, pp. 5-6.

163. *Ibid*, p. 40.

164. *Ibid*, p. 36.

165. *Ibid*, p. 36.

166. *Ibid*, p. 36.

167. *Ibid*, p. 37.

168. Prigge and Kessler, *supra*, n.153, pp. 282-283.

169. Donald Rothberg, *supra*, n. 6, p.192.

170. Paul Griffiths, "Pure Consciousness and Indian Buddhism" in *The Problem of Pure Consciousness, supra*, n. 5, p. 87.

171. Philip Almond, *supra*, n. 22, p. 218.

172. Robert K.C. Forman, *supra*, n.12, p. 8.

173. *Ibid*, p. 75.

174. *Ibid*, p.183.

175. *Ibid*, p. 295.

176. *Ibid*, p. 220.

177. Steven Katz, *supra*, n.14, p. 46.

178. Evelyn Underhill, *supra*, n. 25, p.158.

179. R.C. Zaehner, *supra*, n. 29, pp.170-174.

180. Robert Gimello, *supra*, n. 31, pp.182-183.

181. Norman Prigge and Gary Kessler, *supra*, n.153, p. 280.

182. Gershom Scholem, *supra*, n. 26, pp.15-16.

183. F.C. Happold, *supra*, n.1, p. 29.

184. Robert K.C. Forman, *supra*, n.12, pp.19-20.

185. F.C. Happold, *supra*, n.1, p. 275.

186. W.T. Stace, *supra*, n. 4, pp.113 & 244.

187. *Ibid*, p.112.

188. *Ibid*, p.119.

189. Evelyn Underhill, *supra*, n. 25, p.167.

190. Nelson Pike, *Mystic Union, An Essay in the Phenomenology of Mysticism*, Cornell University Press, 1992, p. 36-37.

191. *Ibid*, p. 39.

192. *Ibid*, p. 37

193. Prigge and Kessler, *supra*, n.153, pp. 277-278.

194. F.C. Happold, *supra*, n.1, pp.107-108.

118

195. S.N. Dasgupta, *supra*, n. 2, pp.102-109.

196. Robert Gimello, *supra*, n. 31, p.194.

197. Evelyn Underhill, *supra*, n. 25, p. 61.

198. *Ibid*, p.178.

199. Frits Staal, *supra*, n.138, pp. 54-55.

200. W.T. Stace, *supra*, n. 4, p.143.

201. *Ibid*, pp.144-145.

202. *Ibid*, p.198.

203. Brian Fay, *Contemporary Philosophy of Social Science*, Blackwell Publishers, 1996, p. 201.

204. *Ibid,* p. 201.

205. *Ibid*, p. 201.

206. *Ibid*, p. 202.

207. *Ibid,* p. 204.

208. *Ibid*, p. 213.

209. J.N. Findlay, *supra*, n. 24, p.180-181.

210. W.T. Stace, *supra*, n. 4, p. 206.

211. Evelyn Underhill, *supra*, n. 25, pp. 28-29.

212. *Ibid*, pp.168-169.

213. *Ibid*, p.178.

214. Russell, *supra*, n. 3, p.18

Bibliography

Chuang-Tzu, *Chuang Tzu Basic Writings*, Columbia University Press, 1964, translated by Burton Watson.

Dasgupta, S.N., *Hindu Mysticism*, Motilal Banarsidass, 1927.

Fay, Brian, *Contemporary Philosophy of Social Science*, Blackwell Publishers, 1996.

Findlay, J.N., *Ascent to the Absolute*, Humanities Press, 1970.

Foreman, Robert, editor, *The Problem of Pure Consciousness*, Oxford University Press, 1990.

Foster, Nelson and Shoemaker, Jack, *The Roaring Stream*, The Ecco Press, 1996.

Happold, F.C., *Mysticism*, Penguin Books, 1963.

James, William, *The Varieties of Religious Experience*, 1902, Touchstone: Simon and Schuster, 1997.

Katz, Steven T., editor, *Mysticism and Philosophical Analysis*, Oxford University Press, 1978.

Katz, Steven T., editor, *Mysticism and Religious Traditions*, Oxford University Press, 1983.

Lao-Tzu, *Tao Te Ching*, Alfred A. Knopf, Everyman's Library, 1994, edited by Sarah Allan, T. Ching, translation by D.C. Lau.

Matt, Daniel, *The Essential Kabbalah*, Castle Books, 1995.

Pike, Nelson, *Mystic Union, An Essay in the Phenomenology of Mysticism*, Cornell University Press, 1992.

Russell, Bertrand, *Mysticism and Philosophy*, Penguin Books, 1918.

Scholem, Gershom, *On the Kabbalah and Its Symbolism*, Schocken Books, 1965.

Staal, Frits, *Exploring Mysticism: A Methodological Essay*, University of California Press, 1976.

Stace, W.T., *Mysticism and Philosophy*, London: Macmillan Press, 1960.

Underhill, Evelyn, *Practical Mysticism*, Ariel Press, 1914.

Zaehner, R.C., *Sacred and Profane*, Clarendon Press, 1957; Oxford University Press, 1961.

Index